Creating Web Applications with Ruby on Rails: A Developer's Guide

A Step-by-Step Guide to Mastering Ruby on Rails for Web Development

BOOZMAN RICHARD

BOOKER BLUNT

Table of Content

TABLE OF CONTENTS

INTRODUCTION

Mastering Ruby on Rails – A Comprehensive Guide to Building Scalable Web Applications

Welcome to **"Mastering Ruby on Rails"**, your ultimate guide to learning and mastering Rails, one of the most powerful and versatile web application frameworks available today. Whether you're a beginner just getting started with Rails or an experienced developer looking to sharpen your skills, this book is designed to provide you with a comprehensive understanding of the Rails framework and how to effectively use it to build scalable, maintainable, and high-performing web applications.

Ruby on Rails, often referred to simply as **Rails**, has become a popular choice for developers building web applications due to its simplicity, speed, and emphasis on convention over configuration. Rails allows developers to focus on building features and functionality rather than worrying about the complexities of the underlying architecture. With an active community, a wealth of resources, and a solid ecosystem of gems and tools, Rails is a framework that has powered everything from small startup websites to massive, high-traffic platforms.

This book covers everything you need to know to become a proficient Rails developer. From the basics of setting up a Rails project and understanding the Model-View-Controller (MVC) architecture to deploying a fully-functional, production-ready application, we'll walk through every essential aspect of Rails development.

What You Will Learn in This Book

This book is divided into 24 chapters, each focusing on a different aspect of Rails development, with practical examples and step-by-step instructions to ensure you gain hands-on experience. Here's what you can expect to learn:

1. **Getting Started with Rails**: You'll begin by setting up your development environment, creating your first Rails application, and understanding the foundational concepts that make Rails such an efficient framework.

2. **MVC Architecture**: We'll dive into the **Model-View-Controller (MVC)** architecture, which is the

heart of Rails. You'll learn how Rails implements MVC and how to structure your application to follow this pattern, ensuring your code is maintainable and scalable.

3. **Working with Databases**: As a web framework, Rails is deeply tied to databases. You'll learn how to use **ActiveRecord**, Rails' Object-Relational Mapping (ORM) system, to interact with your database, manage migrations, and handle database relationships.

4. **Authentication and Authorization**: Security is crucial in any web application. In this book, we'll cover how to implement secure user authentication, manage user roles, and integrate third-party authentication services like OAuth.

5. **Building APIs**: In today's world, many applications need to interact with other services and platforms via APIs. You'll learn how to build and consume **RESTful APIs** in Rails, handling JSON responses, and making your application more modular and service-oriented.

6. **Performance Optimization**: We'll explore techniques for **scaling** and improving the **performance** of your Rails applications, from

database optimizations to caching strategies and load balancing.

7. **Testing and Debugging**: Rails is built with testing in mind, and we'll show you how to write automated tests to ensure the quality and reliability of your code. You'll learn about the Rails testing framework, the importance of Test-Driven Development (TDD), and how to handle common bugs and errors.

8. **Deployment**: After building your application, it's time to deploy it for the world to see. We'll cover various deployment methods, including **Heroku**, **AWS**, and **DigitalOcean**, so you can choose the best platform for your application.

9. **Security Best Practices**: Security is paramount in modern web applications. This book will cover essential **security practices** to safeguard your application from threats like **SQL injection, Cross-Site Scripting (XSS)**, and **Cross-Site Request Forgery (CSRF)**.

10. **Advanced Topics**: We'll dive deeper into advanced topics like **service objects, POROs (Plain Old Ruby Objects), background jobs**, and **real-time applications**. These patterns and techniques are

essential for building complex, high-performance Rails applications.

11. **Collaborating with Git and GitHub**: Collaboration is essential in modern software development, and we'll cover how to use **Git** and **GitHub** to manage your code, work with teams, and implement best practices for version control.

12. **The Future of Rails**: Finally, we'll explore the **future of Rails**, including upcoming features in **Rails 7** and beyond, and how to contribute to the vibrant Rails community.

Why This Book Is Different

Rails is a powerful framework, but it can sometimes be overwhelming for new developers. This book is structured to break down complex topics into digestible sections, each with practical examples and real-world applications. You'll gain more than just theoretical knowledge; you'll learn by **building real applications**, solving common problems, and gaining a deeper understanding of Rails.

- **Hands-on Examples**: Throughout the book, you'll build a fully functional Rails application, with each chapter adding new features and functionality.
- **Clear, Concise Explanations**: We avoid unnecessary jargon and focus on clear, straightforward explanations that make complex concepts easy to understand.
- **Up-to-Date with Rails 7**: This book is fully up-to-date with the latest version of Rails, ensuring that you are learning the most relevant and modern techniques.
- **Practical Tools for Collaboration**: Whether you're working solo or as part of a team, we'll teach you how to use **version control** and **collaboration tools** effectively to manage your code and collaborate on projects.

Who Should Read This Book?

This book is designed for developers of all experience levels. Whether you're just starting with Ruby on Rails or looking to level up your existing skills, this guide will help you master the key concepts and best practices that every Rails developer needs to know.

- **Beginners**: If you're new to web development, this book will walk you through the basics, starting with the foundations of Rails and gradually introducing more advanced concepts as you build your skills.
- **Intermediate Developers**: If you're already familiar with Rails but want to improve your understanding of advanced topics like performance optimization, background jobs, or API development, this book will help you deepen your knowledge.
- **Experienced Developers**: For those who are already proficient in Rails, this book will provide valuable insights into best practices, new features in Rails 7, and how to scale and optimize your application for production.

Get Ready to Build Powerful Applications

By the end of this book, you'll have all the knowledge and tools you need to **build scalable, high-performance web applications** with Ruby on Rails. Whether you're working on a personal project or collaborating on a large-scale enterprise application, the skills you learn here will serve as a solid foundation for your development journey.

Let's get started with **Mastering Ruby on Rails** and begin building the next great web application today!

CHAPTER 1

INTRODUCTION TO RUBY ON RAILS

Overview of Ruby on Rails: What it is and Why It's Popular

Ruby on Rails, often referred to simply as "Rails," is an open-source web application framework written in Ruby, a dynamic programming language. Rails was designed to simplify web development by providing a set of tools and conventions that allow developers to focus on building the functionality of their applications rather than worrying about repetitive code or complex configurations.

Rails is based on the Model-View-Controller (MVC) architectural pattern, which separates an application into three interconnected components:

- **Model**: Represents the data and the logic of the application.
- **View**: The user interface that displays the data.
- **Controller**: Manages the interaction between the model and view, handling requests and responding to them.

Rails is popular for several reasons:

1. **Speed of Development**: Rails emphasizes convention over configuration (CoC), which means developers don't need to spend time making decisions about the setup and structure of their apps. This leads to faster development and more efficient coding.

2. **Rich Ecosystem**: Rails comes with a wide array of built-in tools and libraries (gems) that streamline many aspects of web development, from authentication to testing.

3. **Scalability**: Despite being known for rapid prototyping, Rails is also capable of handling large-scale applications.

4. **Community Support**: Rails has a vibrant and active community that contributes to a wealth of tutorials, documentation, and libraries.

The Rails Philosophy: Convention over Configuration

One of the defining principles of Rails is **"Convention over Configuration"** (CoC). This philosophy encourages developers to follow common conventions for organizing their code, which reduces the need for configuration. In other words, Rails makes assumptions about what developers want to do and structures the app accordingly.

For example:

- **Naming conventions**: Rails expects models to be named in singular form (e.g., `Post` for a `posts` table in the database) and controllers to be named in plural form (`PostsController`).

- **Folder structure**: Rails automatically knows where to find views, models, and controllers based on the structure of your application.

- **Automatic routing**: With Rails, routes are generated for common resources, so you don't have to manually configure each URL path.

This philosophy saves time and effort and allows developers to work more productively. Since Rails is designed to do the "right thing" by default, it also helps developers avoid common mistakes.

Setting Up Ruby and Rails: Installation and Environment Setup

Before you start building applications with Rails, you'll need to set up your development environment. Here's a step-by-step guide to getting Ruby and Rails up and running on your machine:

1. **Install Ruby**: Ruby is the programming language that Rails is built on, so you'll need to have Ruby installed on your system. The easiest way to install Ruby is through **RVM** (Ruby Version Manager) or **rbenv**.

- o **RVM Installation** (for macOS and Linux):

```
pgsql
```

```
\curl -sSL https://get.rvm.io | bash
-s stable
```

- o After installing RVM, you can install Ruby by running:

```
nginx
```

```
rvm install ruby
```

2. **Install Rails**: Once Ruby is installed, you can install Rails using the Ruby gem system:

```
nginx
```

```
gem install rails
```

This will install the latest stable version of Rails and all the dependencies required for running Rails applications.

3. **Check the Installation**: After installing Ruby and Rails, you can verify their installation by running:

```
nginx
```

```
ruby -v
```

```
rails -v
```

These commands should display the installed versions of Ruby and Rails.

4. **Install a Database**: Rails uses a database to store and manage data. By default, Rails works with SQLite, which comes preconfigured, but you can also use other databases like PostgreSQL or MySQL.
   - o For **SQLite**, you don't need to do anything extra. Rails will use it out of the box.
   - o For **PostgreSQL** or **MySQL**, you'll need to install the database software separately and configure your Rails application to use it.

5. **Set Up Your Text Editor**: Choose a text editor or Integrated Development Environment (IDE) for writing your code. Popular choices include:
   - o **VS Code** (Visual Studio Code)
   - o **Sublime Text**
   - o **RubyMine** (a dedicated Ruby IDE)

Your First "Hello, World!" App: Creating a Basic Rails App

Now that your environment is set up, let's create a simple "Hello, World!" application to test everything.

1. **Create a New Rails Application**: Open your terminal and run the following command to generate a new Rails app:

```cpp
```

```
rails new hello_world_app
```

This will create a new directory called `hello_world_app` with all the necessary files and folders for a Rails application.

2. **Navigate to the Application Directory**:

```bash
```

```
cd hello_world_app
```

3. **Start the Rails Development Server**: Rails comes with a built-in server that you can use to run your application locally. Start it by running:

```nginx
```

```
rails server
```

This will start a web server at `http://localhost:3000`.

4. **Create a Controller and View**: To display "Hello, World!" on the web page, you need a controller and a view.

   o   Generate a controller called `welcome`:

   ```perl
   rails generate controller welcome index
   ```

   o   This will create a `welcome_controller.rb` file and a view for the `index` action.

5. **Edit the View**: Open the generated `app/views/welcome/index.html.erb` file and replace the content with:

   ```html
   <h1>Hello, World!</h1>
   ```

6. **Update the Routes**: Open `config/routes.rb` and update the root route to point to the `index` action of the `welcome` controller:

   ```ruby
   root 'welcome#index'
   ```

21

7. **Visit Your Application**: Go to `http://localhost:3000` in your browser, and you should see "Hello, World!" displayed on the page.

Congratulations! You've successfully created your first Rails application. This simple example illustrates the basic structure of a Rails app, including controllers, views, and routes.

In this chapter, you learned the basics of what Ruby on Rails is, how to set up your development environment, and how to create a basic Rails application. In the following chapters, you'll dive deeper into each part of Rails and learn how to build more complex applications.

CHAPTER 2

UNDERSTANDING MVC ARCHITECTURE

What is MVC?: Breaking Down Model-View-Controller

MVC stands for **Model-View-Controller**, which is a widely used software architectural pattern for developing web applications. It divides an application into three interconnected components, each with a specific role:

1. **Model**:
   - The model represents the application's data and the logic that manipulates it. It is responsible for retrieving, storing, and validating data in the database.
   - The model is also where the business logic resides, meaning it handles all the logic related to managing the data, such as calculations or ensuring data integrity.
   - In Rails, models are typically represented by classes that inherit from `ActiveRecord::Base`, allowing them to interact with the database using ActiveRecord.

23

2. **View**:

   o The view is responsible for displaying the data to the user. It represents the user interface (UI) of the application.

   o Views are typically composed of HTML, CSS, and JavaScript, and in Rails, they are written in **Embedded Ruby (ERB)**, which allows Ruby code to be embedded within HTML.

   o Views are typically located in the `app/views` directory of your Rails application.

3. **Controller**:

   o The controller is the intermediary between the model and the view. It receives user input (such as requests) and decides what to do with that input.

   o The controller fetches the necessary data from the model and passes it to the view for rendering. It also handles user actions, such as form submissions or button clicks.

   o In Rails, controllers are defined as classes that inherit from `ApplicationController`, and each controller typically corresponds to a resource (like `PostsController` for managing blog posts).

The MVC pattern allows for a clean separation of concerns, making the application easier to maintain, scale, and test. It keeps the business logic separate from the user interface, which makes it easier to modify either part without affecting the other.

How Rails Implements MVC: Explanation with Examples

Rails follows the MVC architecture to structure web applications. Below is a breakdown of how Rails implements each part of MVC.

1. **Model**:
   - In Rails, the **model** is typically a class that inherits from `ActiveRecord::Base`, which is an abstraction that helps interact with the database. The model handles database queries, data validation, and business logic.

   For example, a `Post` model in a blog application might look like this:

   ruby

   ```
   class Post < ApplicationRecord
     validates :title, presence: true
     validates :content, presence: true
   end
   ```

o   This `Post` model will automatically map to a `posts` table in the database due to Rails' convention over configuration approach. Rails automatically generates fields like `title` and `content` based on the attributes defined in the model.

2. **View**:

o   The **view** is where the user interface is rendered. In Rails, views are typically written in **ERB (Embedded Ruby)**, which allows Ruby code to be embedded inside HTML.

For example, the view for displaying a list of blog posts might look like this:

```erb
<h1>All Posts</h1>
<ul>
  <% @posts.each do |post| %>
    <li>
      <h2><%= post.title %></h2>
      <p><%= post.content %></p>
    </li>
  <% end %>
</ul>
```

- Here, the `<%= %>` syntax is used to embed Ruby expressions within HTML. The `@posts` variable is an instance variable populated by the controller, which is passed to the view to render the list of posts.

3. **Controller**:

   - The **controller** in Rails is responsible for handling user requests, interacting with models, and passing data to the view. Each controller corresponds to a resource (such as `PostsController` for managing posts), and each controller action represents a different task (such as showing, creating, or editing a post).

   For example, a `PostsController` might look like this:

   ruby

   ```ruby
   class          PostsController          <
   ApplicationController
     def index
       @posts = Post.all
     end

     def show
       @post = Post.find(params[:id])
     end
   end
   ```

o In the `index` action, the controller fetches all the posts from the database using `Post.all` and passes them to the view. In the `show` action, it retrieves a single post based on the ID provided in the URL (`params[:id]`) and passes it to the view.

Each part of the Rails MVC framework works together to create a smooth and organized development experience. The model manages data, the view displays it, and the controller acts as the middleman between the two.

Creating a Simple App: Building a Basic App Using MVC

Let's create a simple blog application to see how MVC works in action. In this example, we will build a basic app that allows users to view a list of blog posts and view individual posts.

1. **Step 1: Set up the Rails Application**

   First, create a new Rails application:

   bash

```bash
rails new blog_app
cd blog_app
```

2. **Step 2: Generate the Post Model**

Generate a `Post` model with `title` and `content` fields:

bash

```
rails generate model Post title:string
content:text
```

This will generate a model, a migration to create the `posts` table, and other associated files. Run the migration to create the database table:

bash

```
rails db:migrate
```

3. **Step 3: Generate the Posts Controller**

Now, generate a controller for posts:

bash

```
rails generate controller Posts index show
```

This will create a `PostsController` with two actions: `index` and `show`. It will also generate corresponding views for each action.

4. **Step 4: Define the Controller Actions**

Open `app/controllers/posts_controller.rb` and modify it as follows:

```ruby
class PostsController < ApplicationController
  def index
    @posts = Post.all
  end

  def show
    @post = Post.find(params[:id])
  end
end
```

In the `index` action, we retrieve all the posts from the database, and in the `show` action, we retrieve a single post by its ID.

5. **Step 5: Create the Views**

Open `app/views/posts/index.html.erb` and add the following code:

```erb
<h1>All Posts</h1>
<ul>
```

```
<% @posts.each do |post| %>
  <li><%=      link_to      post.title,
post_path(post) %></li>
  <% end %>
</ul>
```

This will display a list of all the blog posts. Each title will be a clickable link that directs the user to the individual post's page.

Now, open `app/views/posts/show.html.erb` and add the following code:

erb

```
<h1><%= @post.title %></h1>
<p><%= @post.content %></p>
```

This will display the title and content of the individual post when a user clicks on a post title from the list.

6. **Step 6: Define the Routes**

Open `config/routes.rb` and define the routes for the `index` and `show` actions:

ruby

```
Rails.application.routes.draw do
```

```
resources :posts, only: [:index, :show]
end
```

This generates the necessary routes for displaying the list of posts (index) and individual post details (show).

7. **Step 7: Run the Application**

Start the Rails server:

```
bash
```

```
rails server
```

Visit http://localhost:3000/posts in your browser to see the list of posts. Click on a title to view the individual post.

In this chapter, we covered the **Model-View-Controller** (MVC) architecture and how Rails implements it. We also created a simple blog application using MVC principles, demonstrating how the model handles data, the controller manages the logic, and the view displays the user interface. In the next chapter, we'll dive deeper into Rails' routing system, which helps define how URLs are handled and connected to controller actions.

32

CHAPTER 3

ROUTING AND CONTROLLERS

What is Routing in Rails?

Routing in Rails is the mechanism that maps **HTTP requests** (like a user visiting a webpage) to specific **controller actions**. In Rails, routes are defined in the `config/routes.rb` file. This file tells Rails what to do when a particular URL pattern is accessed. The primary role of routing is to connect a URL request to the appropriate controller and action that should handle the request.

When a user visits a URL, Rails looks through the routes defined in this file to determine which controller and action should handle the request. Rails uses regular expressions to define these URL patterns, making it flexible for developers to define how their app should respond to different types of requests.

For example:

- **HTTP GET** requests are used for retrieving resources, such as displaying a list of blog posts or viewing a single post.
- **HTTP POST** requests are used to submit data, like creating a new post.

- **HTTP PUT/PATCH** requests are used to update data.
- **HTTP DELETE** requests are used to remove resources.

Rails handles these requests through **RESTful routing**, which is a set of conventions that align HTTP methods with CRUD (Create, Read, Update, Delete) actions.

Defining Routes: Setting Up URL Patterns and Linking Them to Actions

In Rails, routes are defined inside the `config/routes.rb` file. This file maps URL patterns to controller actions. You can define routes for specific resources (like posts, users, or comments) or for custom URLs that don't follow the conventional structure.

Here's how you define routes in Rails:

1. **Defining a Route for a Simple Action**: To define a simple route, you specify the URL pattern and the corresponding controller and action. For example:

```ruby
get 'about', to: 'pages#about'
```

- o This route tells Rails that when a user visits `/about`, the `about` action in the `PagesController` should be executed.

2. **Defining RESTful Routes**: For a resource like `posts`, you can define RESTful routes using the `resources` keyword, which automatically creates the standard CRUD routes:

ruby

```
resources. :posts
```

- o This line creates the following routes:
  - GET `/posts` → `posts#index` (view all posts)
  - GET `/posts/new` → `posts#new` (show the form for creating a new post)
  - POST `/posts` → `posts#create` (create a new post)
  - GET `/posts/:id` → `posts#show` (view a single post)
  - GET `/posts/:id/edit` → `posts#edit` (show the form for editing a post)
  - PATCH/PUT `/posts/:id` → `posts#update` (update a post)

- DELETE   `/posts/:id`   →

  `posts#destroy` (delete a post)

These routes adhere to the **RESTful conventions**, making your code clean and easy to maintain.

3. **Custom Routes**: Sometimes, you may need to define custom routes for non-standard actions. For example, to create a route for a `contact` page:

ruby

```
get 'contact', to: 'pages#contact'
```

4. **Named Routes**: Rails allows you to create **named routes** that make generating URLs more readable:

ruby

```
get 'about', to: 'pages#about', as: 'about'
```

- You can now generate the URL for this route with the helper `about_path`.

Controller Actions and Views: A Practical Guide

When a route is hit, Rails calls a specific **controller action**. A **controller** is a Ruby class that processes incoming requests, interacts with the model to retrieve or manipulate data, and then sends the result to a **view** to be rendered.

1. **Controller Actions**: Each controller action is a method defined in a controller class. For example, in a `PostsController`, the `index` action could look like this:

ruby

```
class            PostsController            <
ApplicationController
  def index
    @posts = Post.all
  end

  def show
    @post = Post.find(params[:id])
  end
end
```

- o In the `index` action, we retrieve all the posts from the database and assign them to the `@posts` instance variable.
- o In the `show` action, we retrieve a single post based on its `id` and assign it to `@post`.

2. **Passing Data to Views**: In Rails, controllers pass data to views using **instance variables**. These variables are

37

available in the corresponding view templates (e.g., .html.erb files).

For example, in the index.html.erb view for displaying posts:

erb

```
<h1>All Posts</h1>
<ul>
  <% @posts.each do |post| %>
    <li><%=      link_to       post.title,
post_path(post) %></li>
  <% end %>
</ul>
```

- o The @posts instance variable is used to render a list of all posts. The link_to helper generates a clickable link for each post, which redirects to the individual post's page.

3. **Rendering a View**: By default, Rails will automatically look for a view with the same name as the action. For example, when the index action is executed in the PostsController, Rails will look for a view in app/views/posts/index.html.erb.

You can also explicitly render a view from an action using the render method:

38

```ruby

render 'posts/index'
```

Handling Form Submissions: Creating and Processing Forms in Controllers

Forms are a common part of web applications, whether for creating a new resource (like a post) or updating an existing one. In Rails, handling form submissions involves both creating a form in the view and processing the form data in the controller.

1. **Creating a Form**: Rails provides form helpers to make it easier to build forms. For example, to create a form for submitting a new post, you can use the `form_with` helper:

```erb

<%= form_with model: @post, local: true do
|form| %>
  <%= form.label :title %>
  <%= form.text_field :title %>

  <%= form.label :content %>
  <%= form.text_area :content %>

  <%= form.submit 'Create Post' %>
```

```
<% end %>
```

- o This form generates fields for `title` and `content` and submits the data to the `create` action in the `PostsController`.

2. **Processing the Form in the Controller**: The controller handles the form submission and processes the data. For example, the `create` action in the `PostsController` might look like this:

ruby

```
class          PostsController          <
ApplicationController
  def create
    @post = Post.new(post_params)
    if @post.save
      redirect_to @post, notice: 'Post was
successfully created.'
    else
      render :new
    end
  end

  private

  def post_params
    params.require(:post).permit(:title,
:content)
```

```
end
end
```

    o   The `create` action instantiates a new `Post` object with the data submitted via the form (`post_params`). If the post is saved successfully, the user is redirected to the newly created post's page. If the save fails (e.g., due to validation errors), the form is re-rendered.

3. **Displaying Validation Errors**: If the model has validation errors, you can display them in the view like this:

```
erb
```

```erb
<% if @post.errors.any? %>
  <ul>
    <% @post.errors.full_messages.each do
|message| %>
      <li><%= message %></li>
    <% end %>
  </ul>
<% end %>
```

Summary

In this chapter, we explored how **routing** and **controllers** work together in Rails to handle web requests and manage user interactions. We learned how to define routes, associate them with controller actions, and pass data from the controller to the view. Additionally, we covered how to create and process forms in Rails, handling form submissions with ease using Rails' built-in helpers and conventions. With this understanding, you're now ready to build more dynamic and interactive applications in Rails.

CHAPTER 4

WORKING WITH DATABASES

Rails and Databases: Setting Up Your Database

In a web application, the **database** is used to store and retrieve data. Rails makes it easy to interact with databases by providing an Object-Relational Mapping (ORM) system called **ActiveRecord**. ActiveRecord abstracts the database layer, allowing you to interact with your data using Ruby code instead of writing raw SQL queries.

When you first create a Rails application, Rails will automatically set up a default database configuration using **SQLite** for development and testing environments. For production, you can configure it to use other databases like **PostgreSQL** or **MySQL**.

Here's how you set up the database in a new Rails application:

1. **Configure the Database**: In `config/database.yml`, Rails configures the database connection for different environments (development, test, production). You may need to modify this configuration depending on which database you're using (e.g., PostgreSQL or MySQL).

2. **Create the Database**: Once you've configured your database, you can create the database using the following command:

```bash
rails db:create
```

This will create the database based on the configuration in `database.yml`.

3. **Checking the Connection**: After setting up the database, you can check the connection by running the Rails server:

```bash
rails server
```

This will start the development server and allow you to check if the database is set up correctly.

Rails also comes with a feature for automatic migrations (discussed below) that can be used to create or modify your database schema.

Migrations: Creating, Modifying, and Rolling Back Database Schema

In Rails, **migrations** are used to modify the structure of the database over time. Migrations help you evolve your database schema by adding, removing, or changing columns, tables, and indexes.

1. **Creating Migrations**: To create a migration, you can run the following command:

    bash

    ```
    rails generate migration AddTitleToPosts
    title:string
    ```

    This generates a migration file that adds a `title` column of type `string` to the `posts` table.

2. **Running Migrations**: Once you've created a migration, you can apply it to your database using:

    bash

    ```
    rails db:migrate
    ```

    This will execute all pending migrations and modify your database schema accordingly.

3. **Modifying a Migration**: Migrations can be edited if you need to make changes. For example, if you want to change the type of a column, you can edit the migration file to reflect the changes and re-run the migration.

4. **Rolling Back Migrations**: If something goes wrong or you want to undo a migration, Rails provides a way to **roll back** the last migration:

    ```bash
    bash
    ```

    ```bash
    rails db:rollback
    ```

    You can also specify how many steps to roll back:

    ```bash
    bash
    ```

    ```bash
    rails db:rollback STEP=1
    ```

    This is useful for undoing changes that you no longer need or that caused issues.

5. **Example of a Migration File**: A typical migration file looks like this:

    ```ruby
    ruby
    ```

    ```ruby
    class          AddTitleToPosts          <
    ActiveRecord::Migration[6.0]
      def change
    ```

```
    add_column :posts, :title, :string
  end
end
```

The `change` method defines the database modification, in this case, adding a `title` column to the `posts` table. You can also use methods like `remove_column`, `rename_column`, `add_index`, etc., depending on the changes you want to make.

ActiveRecord Basics: Interacting with Your Database Using ActiveRecord

ActiveRecord is Rails' ORM (Object-Relational Mapping) system that allows you to interact with your database through Ruby objects instead of SQL queries. It provides a set of methods that simplify common database operations like retrieving, creating, updating, and deleting records.

1. **Creating Records**: To create a new record, you can use the `create` method. For example, to create a new `Post` record:

```ruby
post = Post.create(title: "My First Post",
content: "This is the content of my post.")
```

This will insert a new row into the `posts` table with the specified attributes.

2. **Finding Records**: ActiveRecord provides several ways to find records from the database:

   o `Post.find(id)`: Finds a post by its primary key (`id`).

   o `Post.where(attribute: value)`: Finds all posts with the given attribute value.

   o `Post.first`: Retrieves the first post in the table.

   o `Post.last`: Retrieves the last post in the table.

Example:

```ruby
post = Post.find(1)
```

3. **Updating Records**: You can update an existing record by modifying its attributes and calling `save`:

```ruby
post = Post.find(1)
post.title = "Updated Title"
post.save
```

Alternatively, you can use `update` to modify and save the record in one step:

```ruby
ruby
```

```ruby
post.update(title: "Updated Title")
```

4. **Deleting Records**: To delete a record from the database:

```ruby
ruby
```

```ruby
post = Post.find(1)
post.destroy
```

You can also delete all records matching a condition:

```ruby
ruby
```

```ruby
Post.where(content:                    "Old
Content").destroy_all
```

5. **ActiveRecord Queries**: ActiveRecord makes it easy to perform complex queries. For example:

   o `Post.where("created_at   >   ?",
     Time.now - 1.week)`: Find all posts created in the last week.

   o `Post.order(:created_at)`: Get all posts ordered by their creation date.

   o `Post.limit(5)`: Limit the number of records returned to 5.

ActiveRecord automatically handles all the SQL for these operations, so developers don't have to write raw SQL queries manually.

Associations: One-to-many, Many-to-many, and Has_many Relationships

One of the core features of ActiveRecord is its ability to set up **associations** between models. These associations define how models are related to one another and allow you to easily interact with related records.

1. **One-to-Many Association**: A **one-to-many** relationship exists when one record in a model is associated with many records in another model. For example, one `Post` can have many `Comments`.

    o In the `Post` model:

    ```ruby
    ruby
    ```

    ```ruby
    class Post < ApplicationRecord
      has_many :comments
    end
    ```

    o In the `Comment` model:

    ```ruby
    ruby
    ```

```
class Comment < ApplicationRecord
  belongs_to :post
end
```

2. This setup allows you to access all the comments for a post with:

3. ruby

4.

5. post = Post.find(1)

6. comments = post.comments

7. **Many-to-Many Association**: A **many-to-many** relationship occurs when multiple records in one model are related to multiple records in another model. For example, many Students can be enrolled in many Courses.

Rails uses a **join table** to represent many-to-many relationships. Here's how you would set it up:

  o In the Student model:

    ruby

    ```
    class Student < ApplicationRecord
      has_and_belongs_to_many :courses
    end
    ```

  o In the Course model:

51

```ruby
class Course < ApplicationRecord
  has_and_belongs_to_many :students
end
```

Rails automatically creates a join table `students_courses` (with `student_id` and `course_id` columns) to manage this relationship.

8. **Has Many Through Association**: A **has_many :through** relationship is useful when you want to join two models indirectly through a third model. For example, a `Doctor` has many `Patients` through `Appointments`.

   o In the `Doctor` model:

   ```ruby
   class Doctor < ApplicationRecord
     has_many :appointments
     has_many :patients, through: :appointments
   end
   ```

   o In the `Appointment` model:

   ```ruby
   ```

```
class            Appointment         <
ApplicationRecord
  belongs_to :doctor
  belongs_to :patient
end
```

o In the `Patient` model:

```ruby
ruby
```

```
class Patient < ApplicationRecord
  has_many :appointments
  has_many     :doctors,     through:
:appointments
end
```

Summary

In this chapter, we covered the essentials of working with databases in Rails. We learned how to set up your database and perform migrations to manage the schema. We explored how ActiveRecord simplifies database interactions through its powerful methods for creating, reading, updating, and deleting records. Finally, we looked at how Rails handles associations, including one-to-many, many-to-many, and has-many-through relationships, which allow us to represent and interact with complex relationships between data models. With these tools, you can start building dynamic applications that interact with databases seamlessly.

CHAPTER 5

BUILDING MODELS

What Are Models?

In Rails, **models** are the cornerstone of your application's logic and data. A model is a Ruby class that represents an entity in your application and encapsulates the rules for managing that entity's data. Models are responsible for:

- Interacting with the database through **ActiveRecord** (Rails' ORM).
- Enforcing business logic.
- Validating data to ensure integrity.
- Managing relationships between different models (e.g., one-to-many, many-to-many).

A model typically corresponds to a database table (e.g., a `Post` model corresponds to a `posts` table). Each instance of a model represents a single row in that table, and each attribute of the model corresponds to a column in the database.

In Rails, models are placed in the `app/models` directory, and they inherit from `ApplicationRecord` (which in turn inherits from `ActiveRecord::Base`). This inheritance provides them with powerful methods to interact with the database.

Creating Models in Rails: Step-by-Step Guide

Creating a model in Rails is a straightforward process. Here's how you can create a model in Rails step by step.

1. **Generate the Model**: The first step is to generate the model using the Rails generator. Open your terminal and run:

   bash

   ```
   rails generate model Post title:string content:text
   ```

   o This command generates a `Post` model with two attributes: `title` (a string) and `content` (a text field).

   o It also generates a migration file to create the `posts` table with the specified fields.

2. **Check the Generated Files**: After running the generator, Rails creates several files:

   o **Model**: `app/models/post.rb` will be created, which defines the `Post` class.

o **Migration**:
`db/migrate/TIMESTAMP_create_posts.r`
`b` will be created to add the `posts` table to the database.

3. **Run the Migration**: After generating the model, the next step is to run the migration to create the table in the database:

`bash`

`rails db:migrate`

This will create the `posts` table with the `title` and `content` columns.

4. **Check the Model**: Open the generated `app/models/post.rb` file. It should look something like this:

`ruby`

```ruby
class Post < ApplicationRecord
end
```

You can now add any business logic, validations, or relationships to this model.

Validations: Ensuring Data Integrity with Model Validations

In Rails, **validations** are used to ensure that the data stored in the database is accurate and conforms to certain rules. Rails provides a variety of built-in validation methods to check the presence, uniqueness, format, and other conditions of data.

1. **Presence Validation**: You can ensure that a field is not empty by using the `validates_presence_of` or `validates` method:

ruby

```
class Post < ApplicationRecord
  validates :title, presence: true
  validates :content, presence: true
end
```

   o   This ensures that both `title` and `content` must be provided when creating or updating a post.

2. **Uniqueness Validation**: If you need to ensure that a field's value is unique, use the `validates_uniqueness_of` method:

ruby

```
class Post < ApplicationRecord
  validates :title, uniqueness: true
end
```

o   This ensures that no two posts can have the same title.

3. **Length Validation**: You can specify minimum and maximum lengths for a field:

ruby

```
class Post < ApplicationRecord
  validates :title, length: { minimum: 5,
maximum: 100 }
end
```

o   This validates that the title must be between 5 and 100 characters long.

4. **Format Validation**: You can ensure that a field matches a certain regular expression format. For example, to validate an email:

ruby

```
class User < ApplicationRecord
  validates :email, format: { with:
URI::MailTo::EMAIL_REGEXP }
end
```

o   This ensures that the email follows a standard email format.

5. **Custom Validations**: Rails also allows you to create custom validation methods:

```ruby
class Post < ApplicationRecord
  validate :title_must_be_unique

  private

  def title_must_be_unique
    if Post.exists?(title: title)
      errors.add(:title, 'has already been
taken')
    end
  end
end
```

- o This custom validation checks if a post with the same title already exists and adds an error message if it does.

6. **Error Messages**: If any validation fails, an error message is added to the `errors` object. You can display these error messages in the view:

```erb
<% if @post.errors.any? %>
  <ul>
    <% @post.errors.full_messages.each do
|message| %>
      <li><%= message %></li>
```

```
<% end %>
</ul>
<% end %>
```

Validations are a crucial part of ensuring that only valid data is stored in the database and can help prevent data integrity issues.

Callbacks: Working with Before/After Actions in Models

Callbacks in Rails are hooks that allow you to run specific methods at certain points in the lifecycle of an ActiveRecord object (e.g., before or after creating, updating, saving, or destroying a record). Callbacks are useful for performing tasks like data sanitization, logging, or triggering other actions before or after a model object is saved.

1. **Before Callbacks**: A **before callback** runs a method before an action is performed, such as saving or creating a record. For example:

```ruby
class Post < ApplicationRecord
  before_save :capitalize_title

  private

  def capitalize_title
```

61

```
      self.title = title.capitalize
  end
end
```

- o This callback ensures that the title of a post is capitalized before saving it to the database.

2. **After Callbacks**: An **after callback** runs a method after an action is performed, such as after a record is saved or destroyed. For example:

ruby

```
class Post < ApplicationRecord
  after_create :send_notification

  private

  def send_notification
    # Code to send a notification after a
post is created
  end
end
```

- o This callback sends a notification after a new post is created.

3. **Common Callbacks**: Rails provides several common callback methods:
  - o `before_validation`: **Runs before model** validations.

- ○ `after_validation`: Runs after validations but before the object is saved.
- ○ `before_create`: Runs before a record is created.
- ○ `after_create`: Runs after a record is created.
- ○ `before_save`: Runs before a record is saved (either create or update).
- ○ `after_save`: Runs after a record is saved.
- ○ `before_update`: Runs before updating a record.
- ○ `after_update`: Runs after updating a record.
- ○ `before_destroy`: Runs before a record is destroyed.
- ○ `after_destroy`: Runs after a record is destroyed.

4. **Skipping Callbacks**: You can skip callbacks in certain situations using `skip_callback`:

```ruby
ruby

class Post < ApplicationRecord
  before_save :capitalize_title
  skip_callback      :save,      :before,
:capitalize_title,                      if:
:skip_title_capitalization?

  private
```

63

```
def skip_title_capitalization?
    # Logic to decide if title
capitalization should be skipped
    false
  end
end
```

Callbacks are powerful tools that let you hook into the ActiveRecord lifecycle, allowing you to perform operations at specific moments during the model's lifecycle.

Summary

In this chapter, we explored the essentials of **models** in Rails. We covered how to create models, enforce **validations** to ensure data integrity, and use **callbacks** to perform actions before or after certain database operations. Models are the backbone of your application, managing data and implementing business logic. By using validations, you ensure that the data stored in your database meets specific criteria, and callbacks allow you to hook into the lifecycle of your models, automating common tasks like data manipulation and notifications. These tools are fundamental to building robust, maintainable Rails applications.

CHAPTER 6

MASTERING VIEWS

What is a View in Rails?

In the **Model-View-Controller (MVC)** architecture of Rails, the **view** is responsible for rendering the user interface. It is where the data passed from the controller is displayed to the user in an accessible and meaningful way. A view in Rails is typically an HTML file, but it can also include Ruby code embedded within it, allowing dynamic content to be displayed based on the model data.

Rails uses **Embedded Ruby (ERB)** templates for views. This allows Ruby code to be embedded within an HTML document using special `<%= %>` tags. This dynamic nature makes it easy to present data, accept user input, and display different content depending on the application's state.

Views in Rails are located in the `app/views` directory and are named according to the controller and action they correspond to. For example, a view for displaying all posts would typically be located in `app/views/posts/index.html.erb`.

65

Creating Dynamic Views with Embedded Ruby (ERB)

Embedded Ruby (ERB) is a templating system in Rails that allows you to embed Ruby code inside an HTML document. This means that you can include dynamic data (like a list of posts or a user's name) directly within an HTML page. The syntax is straightforward:

- `<%= %>`: This is used to **output** Ruby code into the view. It evaluates the Ruby code and inserts the result into the HTML.
- `<% %>`: This is used for **control flow**. It does not output anything directly but allows you to run Ruby code (like loops or conditionals).

Let's go through a simple example of how ERB works in a Rails view.

1. **Simple Example**: Imagine you have a `Post` model with `title` and `content`. In the `PostsController`, you might have the following `index` action:

```ruby
def index
  @posts = Post.all
end
```

Now, in your view (`app/views/posts/index.html.erb`), you can loop through all the posts and display their titles and content:

```erb
<h1>All Posts</h1>
<ul>
  <% @posts.each do |post| %>
    <li>
      <h2><%= post.title %></h2>
      <p><%= post.content %></p>
    </li>
  <% end %>
</ul>
```

Here's what happens:

- `<% @posts.each do |post| %>`: This starts a loop through all the posts.
- `<%= post.title %>` and `<%= post.content %>`: These lines output the title and content of each post to the HTML.

This approach allows for dynamically generating HTML content based on data from the model.

Using Partials for Reusability: Keeping Your Code DRY

In Rails, **partials** allow you to break down complex views into smaller, reusable components. A partial is simply a view file that can be rendered within other views, which helps keep your code DRY (Don't Repeat Yourself).

1. **Creating a Partial**: To create a partial, you define a separate `.html.erb` file and give it a name starting with an underscore (_). For example, let's create a partial for displaying the details of a single post: `_post.html.erb`.

   erb

   ```erb
   <!-- _post.html.erb -->
   <div class="post">
     <h2><%= post.title %></h2>
     <p><%= post.content %></p>
   </div>
   ```

2. **Rendering a Partial**: To render this partial in the `index.html.erb` view, you use the `render` method:

   erb

   ```erb
   <h1>All Posts</h1>
   <ul>
     <% @posts.each do |post| %>
   ```

```
<li><%=   render   'post',   post:   post
%></li>
  <% end %>
</ul>
```

- o render 'post', post: post tells Rails to render the _post.html.erb partial and pass the post object to it. The post: post syntax is a way of passing the post variable to the partial so that it can be used inside the partial.

3. **Advantages of Using Partials**:
   - o **Reusability**: You can reuse the same partial across multiple views without rewriting the HTML code.
   - o **Maintainability**: Partials make your views more modular and easier to maintain because smaller components are easier to update.
   - o **Cleaner Views**: Using partials helps avoid bloated, long view files and keeps them organized.

Rendering Collections: Efficiently Displaying Lists of Items

In Rails, rendering collections of objects (e.g., a list of blog posts, comments, or products) is a common task. Rails makes this process efficient and easy with the render method.

1. **Rendering a Collection**: Instead of using a loop manually to render each item in a collection, Rails provides a shorthand for rendering multiple items from a collection. For example, to render all posts with a single line of code:

```erb
<%= render @posts %>
```

By default, Rails looks for a partial named `_post.html.erb` to render each post in the collection. This is equivalent to looping through the `@posts` collection and rendering the `_post.html.erb` partial for each post.

2. **Using a Custom Collection Rendering**: If you want to render a collection but use a different partial for each item, you can specify the partial name explicitly:

```erb
<%= render partial: 'post', collection: @posts %>
```

3. **Passing Local Variables to Partials in Collections**: If you need to pass local variables to each partial in the collection, you can do so like this:

erb

```
<%= render partial: 'post', collection:
@posts, locals: { user: current_user } %>
```

In this example, each `post` partial will have access to both the `post` and `user` variables.

4. **Rendering Nested Collections**: In some cases, you might need to render nested collections. For example, if each post has many comments, you can render the comments for each post within the post's partial:

erb

```
<%= render @posts do |post| %>
  <%= render post.comments %>
<% end %>
```

This renders each post and its associated comments in a nested fashion, ensuring the right context is passed to each part.

Summary

In this chapter, we explored the key aspects of **views** in Rails. We learned how to create **dynamic views** using **Embedded Ruby**

71

(ERB), allowing us to display data from models in an HTML format. We also discussed the concept of **partials**, which help keep your views DRY and reusable, and how they improve the maintainability of your application. Finally, we covered how to efficiently **render collections** of items, simplifying the process of displaying lists, and how to pass local variables and manage nested collections. With these techniques, you can build efficient, maintainable, and dynamic user interfaces in Rails.

CHAPTER 7

FORMS AND HANDLING USER INPUT

Creating Forms in Rails: Basic Form Helpers

Forms are a fundamental part of web applications, and in Rails, you can create forms efficiently using the **form helpers** provided by the framework. These helpers simplify the process of generating HTML form elements, binding them to your model, and handling data submission.

1. **Creating a Form with `form_with`**: The most common form helper in Rails is `form_with`. This helper is used to create forms for both creating and updating records. Here's how you create a form for creating a new post:

    erb

    ```
    <%= form_with model: @post, local: true do
    |form| %>
      <%= form.label :title %>
      <%= form.text_field :title %>

      <%= form.label :content %>
    ```

73

```erb
<%= form.text_area :content %>

<%= form.submit 'Create Post' %>
<% end %>
```

- o form_with binds the form to the @post model, meaning that it will automatically handle the parameters for title and content when the form is submitted.
- o form.label generates the <label> tag, and form.text_field and form.text_area generate the input fields for title and content.
- o form.submit generates a submit button that submits the form.

2. **Creating Forms for Editing Existing Records**: If you want to edit an existing record, the form will be similar, but you need to ensure that the model instance is already populated with the existing data. For example, in the edit.html.erb view:

erb

```erb
<%= form_with model: @post, local: true do |form| %>
  <%= form.label :title %>
  <%= form.text_field :title, value: @post.title %>
```

74

```erb
<%= form.label :content %>
<%= form.text_area :content, value:
@post.content %>

<%= form.submit 'Update Post' %>
<% end %>
```

In this case, the form will be pre-populated with the current values of the @post model.

3. **Handling Nested Forms**: If you have associated models (for example, a Post model with many Comments), you can build nested forms. Rails makes it easy to create forms for nested resources using fields_for. For example:

erb

```erb
<%= form_with model: @post, local: true do
|form| %>
  <%= form.label :title %>
  <%= form.text_field :title %>

  <%= form.label :content %>
  <%= form.text_area :content %>

  <%= form.fields_for :comments do
|comment_form| %>
    <%= comment_form.label :body %>
    <%= comment_form.text_area :body %>
```

```
<% end %>

<%= form.submit 'Create Post' %>
<% end %>
```

In this example, `fields_for` is used to create a form for the associated `comments` of the post.

Form Validations: Validating User Input

To ensure that the data entered by users is correct and complete, **form validations** are essential. Rails provides a simple and powerful way to validate user input both on the client side (via JavaScript) and on the server side (using ActiveRecord validations).

1. **Validating Presence of Fields**: Rails provides a built-in validation called `validates_presence_of` to ensure that a field is not left empty. For example, in the `Post` model:

```ruby
ruby

class Post < ApplicationRecord
  validates :title, presence: true
  validates :content, presence: true
end
```

This will prevent the creation of a post without a title or content.

2. **Length Validation**: You can validate that a field meets a certain length requirement:

```ruby
class Post < ApplicationRecord
  validates :title, length: { minimum: 5,
maximum: 100 }
end
```

o   This ensures that the title is at least 5 characters long and no more than 100 characters.

3. **Uniqueness Validation**: To ensure that a field is unique across the database, you can use the `validates_uniqueness_of` validation:

```ruby
class Post < ApplicationRecord
  validates :title, uniqueness: true
end
```

o   This ensures that no two posts can have the same title.

4. **Numericality Validation**: To ensure that a field contains only numbers, use the `validates_numericality_of` validation:

ruby

```
class Product < ApplicationRecord
  validates :price, numericality: true
end
```

   o   This ensures that the `price` field is a number.

5. **Format Validation**: Rails allows you to use regular expressions to validate the format of a field. For example, to ensure an email address is valid:

ruby

```
class User < ApplicationRecord
  validates :email, format: { with: URI::MailTo::EMAIL_REGEXP }
end
```

6. **Displaying Validation Errors**: If a user submits invalid data, you can display the error messages in the view. Here's how to show error messages in a form:

erb

```
<% if @post.errors.any? %>
```

```
<ul>
  <% @post.errors.full_messages.each do
|message| %>
    <li><%= message %></li>
  <% end %>
</ul>
<% end %>
```

- o This checks if there are any validation errors for the @post object and displays them in an unordered list.

Handling File Uploads: Storing Files with ActiveStorage

In modern web applications, it's common for users to upload files, such as images or documents. Rails makes file handling easy with **ActiveStorage**, a built-in library for managing file uploads and storing them in various cloud storage services like Amazon S3 or locally.

1. **Setting Up ActiveStorage**: To use ActiveStorage, you first need to set it up in your Rails application. Run the following command to install ActiveStorage:

```bash
bash
```

```
rails active_storage:install
```

79

This will generate a migration that creates two tables: `active_storage_blobs` and `active_storage_attachments`.

2. **Run the Migration**: Apply the migration to your database:

```bash
rails db:migrate
```

3. **Attaching Files to Models**: To allow a model to attach files, you need to use the `has_one_attached` or `has_many_attached` method. For example, let's allow the `Post` model to have an attached image:

```ruby
class Post < ApplicationRecord
  has_one_attached :image
end
```

4. **Creating a Form for File Uploads**: In your form, you can create a file upload field using the `file_field` helper:

```erb
```

```erb
<%= form_with model: @post, local: true do
|form| %>
  <%= form.label :title %>
  <%= form.text_field :title %>

  <%= form.label :image %>
  <%= form.file_field :image %>

  <%= form.submit 'Create Post' %>
<% end %>
```

This will create an input field for uploading an image file.

5. **Processing and Displaying Files**: After the file is uploaded, you can process and display it. For example, to display the uploaded image in your view:

erb

```erb
<% if @post.image.attached? %>
  <%= image_tag @post.image %>
<% end %>
```

This checks if an image has been uploaded and, if so, displays it using an img tag.

6. **Storing Files**: ActiveStorage stores uploaded files by default in the storage directory (if you are using local storage). For production environments, you will likely

want to use a cloud storage service like Amazon S3. You can configure this in `config/storage.yml` and set the appropriate environment configuration in `config/environments/production.rb`.

Example of configuring Amazon S3 in `storage.yml`:

yaml

```
amazon:
  service: S3
  access_key_id:                    <%=
ENV['AWS_ACCESS_KEY_ID'] %>
  secret_access_key:                <%=
ENV['AWS_SECRET_ACCESS_KEY'] %>
  bucket: <%= ENV['AWS_BUCKET'] %>
  region: <%= ENV['AWS_REGION'] %>
```

In the production environment (`config/environments/production.rb`):

ruby

```
config.active_storage.service = :amazon
```

Summary

In this chapter, we explored how to create and handle forms in Rails, manage form validations to ensure data integrity, and handle file uploads using **ActiveStorage**. Rails' form helpers make it easy to generate and manage forms, while validations ensure that the user input is correct and meets the necessary requirements. Additionally, ActiveStorage allows you to handle file uploads efficiently and store them in cloud services or locally. These tools are essential for building dynamic, user-interactive applications that handle data and media seamlessly.

CHAPTER 8

WORKING WITH RAILS HELPERS

What Are Helpers?

In Rails, **helpers** are modules that provide methods to assist in rendering views. They allow you to encapsulate reusable code that makes your views cleaner and easier to maintain. Helpers are typically used to perform repetitive tasks such as formatting dates, generating links, or handling complex calculations that need to be displayed on the user interface.

Rails automatically includes some built-in helpers, and you can also create your own custom helpers to extend functionality specific to your application.

Helpers are stored in the `app/helpers` directory, and Rails automatically loads them, making them available to your views. Every view has access to the methods defined in helpers, whether they are built-in or custom.

Built-in Helpers: Working with Rails' Built-in Helpers

Rails comes with a variety of built-in helpers that simplify common tasks in the view. Some of the most commonly used helpers include:

1. **Link Helpers**:
   - `link_to`: Used to generate anchor (`<a>`) tags for creating hyperlinks.

     erb

     ```
     <%= link_to 'Home', root_path %>
     ```

     - This generates a link to the root path of the application with the text "Home."

2. **Form Helpers**:
   - `form_for`: Used to create forms for models.

     erb

     ```
     <%= form_for @post do |f| %>
       <%= f.label :title %>
       <%= f.text_field :title %>
     <% end %>
     ```

     - This generates a form for creating or editing a `Post` model.

85

o `form_with`: **A modern alternative to** `form_for`, **especially in Rails 5.1 and above.**

erb

```
<%= form_with model: @post do |form|
%>
  <%= form.text_field :title %>
<% end %>
```

3. **Number Helpers**:

o `number_to_currency`: **Formats a number as a currency.**

erb

```
<%= number_to_currency(1000) %>
```

- This outputs: `$1,000.00` (formatted based on the locale).

o `number_to_percentage`: **Converts a number into a percentage.**

erb

```
<%=        number_to_percentage(0.75,
precision: 2) %>
```

- This outputs: `75.00%`.

4. **Date and Time Helpers**:

   o `time_ago_in_words`: Displays a timestamp in a human-readable format.

   erb

   ```
   <%=
   time_ago_in_words(@post.created_at)
   %>
   ```

   - This outputs something like "3 days ago."

   o `distance_of_time_in_words`: Calculates the distance between two time points in a human-readable format.

   erb

   ```
   <%=
   distance_of_time_in_words(Time.now,
   @post.created_at) %>
   ```

   - This could output: "about 2 days" or "less than a minute."

5. **Image Helpers**:

   o `image_tag`: Used to generate an image tag in HTML.

   erb

```
<%=    image_tag    'logo.png',    alt:
'Logo' %>
```

- This   outputs: `<img`
  `src="/assets/logo.png"`
  `alt="Logo" />`.

6. **URL Helpers**:

   o `root_path`: Provides a URL to the root path of
      the application.

      erb

      ```
      <%= link_to 'Home', root_path %>
      ```

   o `post_path`: Generates a path to a specific post
      (assuming a `posts` resource).

      erb

      ```
      <%=    link_to    'Show    Post',
      post_path(@post) %>
      ```

7. **Content Helpers**:

   o `pluralize`: Used to convert a singular word to
      plural if necessary.

      erb

```
<%= pluralize(@posts.count, 'post')
%>
```

- This could output: "1 post" or "5 posts" depending on the count.

Creating Your Own Helpers: Customizing Functionality for Views

While Rails provides many built-in helpers, there are often times when you need custom logic specific to your application. In such cases, you can create your own helper methods to make your views more readable and maintainable.

1. **Creating a Custom Helper**: You can define your own helper methods in Rails by creating a module in the app/helpers directory. For example, let's create a helper for formatting post titles.

    o Open the app/helpers/posts_helper.rb file (if it doesn't exist, create it).

    ruby

    ```
    module PostsHelper
      def format_post_title(title)
        title.titleize
      end
    end
    ```

- o This helper defines a method called `format_post_title` that capitalizes the words in the post's title.

2. **Using Your Custom Helper in Views**: After defining the helper method, you can use it in the view like any other method:

erb

```
<h1><%=    format_post_title(@post.title)
%></h1>
```

- o This will display the post title in title case (e.g., "My First Post").

3. **Helper Methods with Parameters**: You can pass arguments to your helper methods to make them more flexible. For example, let's create a helper that formats a given price based on the user's locale:

ruby

```
module ApplicationHelper
  def format_price(price, currency = '$')
    "#{currency}#{'%.2f' % price}"
  end
end
```

- o This helper method takes a `price` and optionally a `currency` symbol. It formats the price to two decimal places and prepends the currency symbol.

4. **Using Your Helper in Views**: Now, you can use the helper method in your views:

erb

```
<%= format_price(99.99) %>
```

- o This will output: `$99.99`.

5. **Helper Methods for Complex Logic**: You can also use helpers to perform more complex logic. For example, let's say we want a helper that determines whether a user has the necessary permissions to edit a post:

ruby

```
module PostsHelper
  def can_edit_post?(user, post)
    user == post.user || user.admin?
  end
end
```

- o This helper checks if the current user is either the author of the post or an admin. You can then use it in your view to conditionally display the "Edit" button:

erb

```
<% if can_edit_post?(current_user,
@post) %>
  <%= link_to 'Edit',
edit_post_path(@post) %>
<% end %>
```

6. **Helper Methods in Application-wide Context**: If you want a helper to be available across all views in the application, define it in `app/helpers/application_helper.rb` (this file is automatically loaded in all views):

ruby

```
module ApplicationHelper
  def full_title(page_title = '')
    base_title = "My Awesome App"
    page_title.empty? ? base_title :
"#{page_title} | #{base_title}"
  end
end
```

o   This helper method can be used across any view to display the full title of the page:

92

```erb
<title><%= full_title('About Us') %></title>
```

o If `page_title` is "About Us", this will output:
   `About Us | My Awesome App.`

Summary

In this chapter, we learned how to use **helpers** in Rails to simplify view rendering. We covered several **built-in helpers** for common tasks like generating links, creating forms, formatting dates and numbers, and displaying images. Rails also allows us to create **custom helpers** to implement application-specific logic, making views more readable and reusable. By creating reusable helper methods, we can ensure that our views remain clean and easy to maintain, and we can centralize complex logic that would otherwise clutter the view templates. With this knowledge, you can create highly dynamic and efficient user interfaces in Rails.

CHAPTER 9

RAILS CONTROLLERS AND RESTFUL ROUTES

The Importance of RESTful Design in Rails

REST (Representational State Transfer) is an architectural style used to design networked applications. In the context of Rails, **RESTful design** refers to the convention of mapping HTTP requests to specific actions in a controller based on the CRUD (Create, Read, Update, Delete) operations. RESTful routing is crucial because it:

1. **Standardizes URL patterns**: RESTful design promotes a consistent and predictable way of defining URLs for resources, making your application easier to understand and maintain.

2. **Aligns with HTTP methods**: RESTful routes take full advantage of HTTP methods (GET, POST, PATCH, DELETE) to map operations on resources. This leads to more intuitive and semantically correct routes.

3. **Promotes resource-based thinking**: RESTful design encourages developers to think of their application in terms of **resources** (such as posts, users, products) and

standardizes how resources are accessed and manipulated through URLs.

For example, with RESTful routing, you create a resource (`Post`) and generate routes that align with the actions you want to perform on the resource. These actions align with HTTP methods:

- **GET /posts** → Index action (list all posts)
- **GET /posts/:id** → Show action (view a single post)
- **POST /posts** → Create action (create a new post)
- **PATCH/PUT /posts/:id** → Update action (edit a post)
- **DELETE /posts/:id** → Destroy action (delete a post)

This approach provides clear and consistent URLs for interacting with your application's resources.

How to Structure Controllers for REST: Practical Examples

In Rails, controllers are responsible for handling the logic of processing requests and providing responses. With RESTful design, controllers are structured to follow standard CRUD actions. Below is an example of how to structure controllers for RESTful resources.

1. **Basic Controller Structure**: A Rails controller typically inherits from `ApplicationController` and contains actions corresponding to the CRUD operations on a

95

model. For example, a `PostsController` could look like this:

```ruby
ruby

class           PostsController              <
ApplicationController
  # GET /posts
  def index
    @posts = Post.all
  end

  # GET /posts/:id
  def show
    @post = Post.find(params[:id])
  end

  # GET /posts/new
  def new
    @post = Post.new
  end

  # POST /posts
  def create
    @post = Post.new(post_params)
    if @post.save
      redirect_to @post, notice: 'Post was
successfully created.'
    else
```

```ruby
      render :new
    end
  end


  # GET /posts/:id/edit
  def edit
    @post = Post.find(params[:id])
  end


  # PATCH/PUT /posts/:id
  def update
    @post = Post.find(params[:id])
    if @post.update(post_params)
      redirect_to @post, notice: 'Post was
successfully updated.'
    else
      render :edit
    end
  end


  # DELETE /posts/:id
  def destroy
    @post = Post.find(params[:id])
    @post.destroy
    redirect_to posts_url, notice: 'Post
was successfully destroyed.'
  end


  private
```

```
# Only allow a list of trusted parameters
through.
  def post_params
    params.require(:post).permit(:title,
:content)
  end
end
```

Explanation:

- o **index**: Displays a list of all posts.
- o **show**: Displays a single post.
- o **new**: Displays a form for creating a new post.
- o **create**: Handles the form submission for creating a new post.
- o **edit**: Displays a form for editing an existing post.
- o **update**: Handles the form submission for updating an existing post.
- o **destroy**: Deletes a specific post.

The controller uses the standard Rails methods to interact with the `Post` model, allowing for clean, RESTful actions.

2. **Controller Action Flow**:
   - o **Index**: Retrieves a list of records (e.g., `Post.all`).

- o **Show**: Retrieves a specific record by ID (e.g., `Post.find(params[:id])`).

- o **Create/Update**: Handles form submissions, creating or updating a resource.

- o **Destroy**: Deletes a resource.

3. **Strong Parameters**: Rails uses **strong parameters** to ensure that only permitted parameters are used in creating or updating resources. The `post_params` method in the controller defines which attributes can be used for `Post`.

Advanced Routing: Custom Routes, Constraints, and Dynamic Segments

In addition to the standard RESTful routes, Rails allows for more complex routing through **custom routes**, **constraints**, and **dynamic segments**. These advanced techniques help when you need to customize URL patterns or add restrictions.

1. **Custom Routes**: Sometimes, you need to define routes that don't fit the RESTful pattern. You can create custom routes to map URLs to controller actions. For example:

```ruby
# config/routes.rb
get 'about', to: 'pages#about'
get 'contact', to: 'pages#contact'
```

This defines custom routes for static pages like "About" and "Contact." You can use custom routes in the same way as RESTful routes, but they don't follow the standard resource-based structure.

2. **Named Routes**: Rails allows you to define **named routes** that make your URL generation easier to understand and maintain:

```ruby
ruby
```

```ruby
get 'posts/:id', to: 'posts#show', as: 'post'
```

This creates a named route `post_path(@post)` for accessing a specific post.

3. **Dynamic Segments**: Dynamic segments allow you to capture parts of the URL to be passed as parameters. For example, consider the following route:

```ruby
ruby
```

```ruby
get 'posts/:id', to: 'posts#show'
```

- o `:id` is a dynamic segment. If you visit `/posts/1`, Rails will pass 1 as `params[:id]` to the `show` action in the `PostsController`.
- o You can also add multiple dynamic segments:

```
ruby
```

```
get    'posts/:year/:month',    to:
'posts#archive'
```

4. **Route Constraints**: **Route constraints** are useful when you want to enforce rules on dynamic segments or restrict access to specific routes based on conditions. For example, to restrict the `:id` parameter to only numbers:

```
ruby
```

```
get    'posts/:id',    to:    'posts#show',
constraints: { id: /\d+/ }
```

This ensures that the `:id` parameter only matches numerical values.

5. **Nested Resources**: Rails allows for **nested routes** to handle relationships between resources. For example, if a post has many comments, you can nest the routes:

```
ruby
```

```
resources :posts do
  resources :comments
end
```

This creates routes like:

- o GET /posts/:post_id/comments →
  comments#index
- o POST /posts/:post_id/comments →
  comments#create
- o GET /posts/:post_id/comments/:id →
  comments#show

The post_id in the nested routes refers to the parent resource, allowing you to organize routes hierarchically.

6. **Root Route**: The root route defines the URL that should be loaded when a user visits the base URL of the application:

```ruby
```

```ruby
root 'home#index'
```

This will load the index action in the HomeController when a user visits the root URL (/).

Summary

In this chapter, we explored the importance of **RESTful design** in Rails and how it leads to consistent, predictable, and maintainable routes for your application. We discussed how to structure controllers for **RESTful actions** (CRUD operations) and how to build controllers that handle requests for resources efficiently. We also covered **advanced routing** techniques, including **custom routes**, **dynamic segments**, **constraints**, and **nested resources**, which allow you to further customize how your application handles requests. By mastering these concepts, you'll be able to create clean, scalable, and flexible routing structures that handle a wide variety of use cases in your Rails applications.

CHAPTER 10

IMPLEMENTING AUTHENTICATION AND AUTHORIZATION

Authentication Basics: Using Gems like Devise

Authentication is the process of verifying the identity of a user. In a typical web application, this means ensuring that the user is who they claim to be, typically by using a combination of a username/email and password. Rails provides several solutions for implementing authentication, with the most popular being the **Devise** gem.

Devise is a flexible and robust authentication solution for Rails. It provides a full suite of features like user registration, login/logout, password recovery, and more, without the need to build these features from scratch.

1. **Installing Devise**: First, add Devise to your Gemfile:

```ruby
gem 'devise'
```

Then, run the following command to install the gem:

```bash
bash
```

```bash
bundle install
```

2. **Setting Up Devise**: After installation, you need to generate the Devise configuration file:

```bash
bash
```

```bash
rails generate devise:install
```

This will create an initializer file (`config/initializers/devise.rb`) and provide important configuration instructions in your terminal.

3. **Creating the User Model**: Now you can generate a model for users. By default, Devise provides common authentication fields such as email, password, and password confirmation. To create a `User` model with Devise, run:

```bash
bash
```

```bash
rails generate devise User
```

This will generate a migration to create a `users` table with the necessary fields, including `email`, encrypted_password,   reset_password_token, and others.

4. **Running the Migration**: Run the migration to create the users table in your database:

bash

```
rails db:migrate
```

5. **Adding Devise Views (Optional)**: Devise comes with a set of pre-built views for handling user registration, login, password reset, etc. To add these views to your application, run:

bash

```
rails generate devise:views
```

This will generate the view files in app/views/devise/, which you can customize to match your application's design.

6. **Using Devise for Authentication**: Now that Devise is set up, you can use its built-in helper methods in your controllers and views. For example, you can use before_action to restrict access to certain pages for authenticated users:

```ruby

class          PostsController          <
ApplicationController
  before_action :authenticate_user!
end
```

This ensures that only logged-in users can access actions in the `PostsController`.

Authorization: Managing User Roles with Pundit or CanCanCan

Authorization refers to determining what actions a user is allowed to perform. While authentication confirms a user's identity, authorization ensures that the authenticated user has the appropriate permissions to perform a specific action, such as accessing a page or modifying data.

Two popular gems for handling authorization in Rails are **Pundit** and **CanCanCan**. These gems provide a framework for defining user roles and controlling access to resources.

1. Using Pundit for Authorization

Pundit is a simple and lightweight gem for managing authorization policies in Rails. It works by defining **policy classes**

107

that control access to specific resources based on the user's role and other conditions.

- **Installing Pundit**: Add Pundit to your Gemfile:

```ruby
gem 'pundit'
```

Then, run:

```bash
bundle install
```

- **Setting Up Pundit**: Generate a policy for a resource (e.g., `Post`):

```bash
rails generate pundit:policy post
```

This will generate a `PostPolicy` class in `app/policies/post_policy.rb`, where you can define the rules for accessing posts.

- **Example of PostPolicy**:

```ruby
```

```
class PostPolicy < ApplicationPolicy
  def show?
    user.admin? || record.user == user
  end

  def create?
    user.present?
  end

  def update?
    user.admin? || record.user == user
  end

  def destroy?
    user.admin?
  end
end
```

In this example:

- o show?: Only admins or the post's author can view a post.

- o create?: Any logged-in user can create a post.

- o update?: Only admins or the post's author can edit a post.

- o destroy?: Only admins can delete a post.

- **Using Pundit in Controllers**: To use Pundit in a controller, you need to call the authorize method before performing an action:

```ruby
class PostsController < ApplicationController
  before_action :authenticate_user!

  def show
    @post = Post.find(params[:id])
    authorize @post
  end
end
```

The `authorize @post` call checks if the current user is allowed to perform the action defined in `PostPolicy`.

2. Using CanCanCan for Authorization

CanCanCan is another popular gem for managing user permissions in Rails. It uses **ability classes** to define user roles and permissions.

- **Installing CanCanCan**: Add CanCanCan to your Gemfile:

```ruby
gem 'cancancan'
```

Then, run:

```
bash
```

```
bundle install
```

- **Setting Up CanCanCan**: You need to define an `Ability` class that contains all the rules for user permissions. To generate this class, run:

```
bash
```

```
rails generate cancan:ability
```

This will create a file `app/models/ability.rb`, where you can define user permissions.

- **Example of Ability Class**:

```ruby
ruby
```

```ruby
class Ability
  include CanCan::Ability

  def initialize(user)
    user ||= User.new # guest user (not logged in)

    if user.admin?
      can :manage, :all
    else
      can :read, Post
```

111

```
      can :create, Post
      can :update, Post, user_id: user.id
      can :destroy, Post, user_id: user.id
    end
  end
end
```

In this example:

- o Admin users have full access to all resources (`can :manage, :all`).
- o Regular users can read and create posts but can only update or destroy posts they own.
- **Using CanCanCan in Controllers**: To check permissions in a controller, use the `authorize!` method:

```ruby
class          PostsController          <
ApplicationController
  before_action :authenticate_user!

  def show
    @post = Post.find(params[:id])
    authorize! :read, @post
  end

  def update
    @post = Post.find(params[:id])
```

```
    authorize! :update, @post
    # Update logic here
  end
end
```

The `authorize! :action, @resource` checks if the current user has permission to perform the specified action (`:read`, `:update`, etc.) on the resource (`@post`).

User Login and Sign-Up: Step-by-Step Guide to Handling User Authentication

Now that we've covered authentication and authorization in general, let's go through the process of **user login** and **sign-up** in Rails using **Devise**.

1. **User Sign-Up**: When a user registers, they will fill out a form with their details (email and password). Devise automatically provides a sign-up form. Here's how to render it in a view:

   erb

   ```
   <%= form_for(@user) do |f| %>
     <%= f.label :email %>
     <%= f.text_field :email %>

     <%= f.label :password %>
   ```

```
<%= f.password_field :password %>

<%= f.submit "Sign Up" %>
<% end %>
```

When the form is submitted, Devise automatically handles the sign-up process and creates a new user.

2. **User Login**: Devise also provides a login form (new_session_path). To render the login form, use:

```
erb

<%=          form_for(:user,          url:
session_path(:user)) do |f| %>
  <%= f.label :email %>
  <%= f.text_field :email %>

  <%= f.label :password %>
  <%= f.password_field :password %>

  <%= f.submit "Log In" %>
<% end %>
```

When the user logs in, Devise checks the credentials and creates a session for the user.

3. **Handling User Logout**: To handle logging out, Devise provides a destroy action. To add a logout link, use:

114

```
erb
```

```
<%=        link_to        'Log        Out',
destroy_user_session_path, method: :delete
%>
```

The `method: :delete` sends a `DELETE` request to the `destroy_user_session_path`, which logs the user out.

Summary

In this chapter, we covered the essential aspects of **authentication** and **authorization** in Rails. We explored how to use **Devise** for managing user authentication, including user sign-up, login, and logout. We also discussed how to manage user permissions and roles using **Pundit** and **CanCanCan** for authorization. By integrating both authentication and authorization, you can ensure that only authorized users can access and modify resources in your application, thus creating a secure and user-friendly environment.

CHAPTER 11

HANDLING ERRORS AND DEBUGGING

Common Rails Errors and How to Fix Them

As with any framework, working with Rails involves encountering errors. Rails provides clear, helpful error messages, which allow developers to quickly understand and resolve issues. Below are some common errors you might encounter in a Rails application and how to fix them.

1. **ActiveRecord::RecordNotFound**
    o **Cause**: This error occurs when you try to find a record in the database that doesn't exist.
    o **Example**:

    ruby

    ```
    @post = Post.find(params[:id])
    ```

    If the post with the given id does not exist, Rails will raise a RecordNotFound exception.

- o **Fix**: Ensure the record exists before attempting to access it. You can use `find_by` instead of `find` to avoid the exception and handle the case where the record is not found:

ruby

```
@post        =        Post.find_by(id:
params[:id])
if @post.nil?
  redirect_to    posts_path,    alert:
"Post not found."
end
```

2. **ActionController::RoutingError**

- o **Cause**: This error occurs when a user tries to access a route that doesn't exist in the `config/routes.rb` file.
- o **Example**: You might get a `RoutingError` when a user tries to visit `/nonexistent_route`.
- o **Fix**: Double-check your `routes.rb` file to make sure the route exists. If you're working with resources, make sure that the correct resources are defined:

ruby

```
resources :posts
```

117

3. **ActiveRecord::StatementInvalid**

   o **Cause**: This error occurs when there is an issue with an SQL query, such as an invalid column name or a problem with data types.

   o **Example**:

   ```ruby
   ```

   ```ruby
   @posts = Post.where('created_at > ?', 'invalid_date')
   ```

   In this case, Rails might attempt to execute an invalid SQL query because the `invalid_date` string is not properly formatted.

   o **Fix**: Ensure that your SQL queries are correct, and that you are passing valid data types for queries. In this case, use a valid date format:

   ```ruby
   ```

   ```ruby
   @posts = Post.where('created_at > ?', Date.today)
   ```

4. **NoMethodError**

   o **Cause**: This error happens when you try to call a method on an object that doesn't respond to that method.

   o **Example**:

118

```ruby
user = nil
user.name
```

- o **Fix**: Make sure that the object you're calling a method on is not `nil`. You can use safe navigation (`&.`) to avoid this error:

```ruby
user&.name
```

5. **ArgumentError**
   - o **Cause**: This error is raised when the number or type of arguments passed to a method is incorrect.
   - o **Example**:

```ruby
def greet(name)
  "Hello, #{name}"
end
greet
```

- o **Fix**: Ensure that you are passing the correct number of arguments to the method:

```ruby
```

```
greet("John")
```

Using the Rails Logger: Debugging Tips and Tricks

One of the most helpful tools for debugging Rails applications is the **Rails logger**. It provides detailed information about the requests, responses, and other events in the application. The log can be found in the `log/development.log` file in development, and `log/production.log` in production.

1. **Basic Logging**: Rails provides several built-in logging methods. The most common are `logger.debug`, `logger.info`, `logger.warn`, and `logger.error`. For example, to log an informational message:

   ruby

   ```
   logger.info "User successfully logged in"
   ```

2. **Logging Query Information**: Rails automatically logs SQL queries, which can help you identify performance bottlenecks. If you want to log a custom query or check the queries made by ActiveRecord:

   ruby

   ```
   @posts = Post.where(title: "Rails").to_a
   ```

120

```
logger.debug "SQL Query: #{@posts.to_sql}"
```

3. **Logging Request and Response Details**: You can also log details about HTTP requests and responses:

ruby

```
logger.debug        "Request        Path:
#{request.path}"
logger.debug        "Response        Status:
#{response.status}"
```

4. **Custom Logging Levels**: Rails supports different log levels to filter messages based on their importance. The log level can be adjusted in the `config/environments/development.rb` or `config/environments/production.rb` file:

ruby

```
config.log_level = :debug
```

o Levels available include `:debug`, `:info`, `:warn`, `:error`, and `:fatal`. In production, you would generally want to set the level to `:info` or `:warn` to avoid verbose logging.

5. **Using the Console for Debugging**: The Rails console is another excellent tool for debugging. You can interact

with your application in an IRB-like environment by running:

```bash
```

```
rails console
```

This allows you to inspect models, check the state of variables, and execute methods in real-time.

6. **Using `pry` for Interactive Debugging**: For a more advanced debugging experience, you can use the `pry` gem, which allows you to stop the execution of your code and inspect variables interactively.

   To install `pry`, add it to your Gemfile:

```ruby
```

```
gem 'pry-rails'
```

   Then, in your code, you can insert:

```ruby
```

```
binding.pry
```

   When the code reaches `binding.pry`, the execution will pause, and you will be able to interact with the current state of your application. You can inspect variables, check the call stack, and run arbitrary Ruby code.

Error Handling in Controllers: How to Handle Exceptions Gracefully

In a production environment, it's crucial to handle errors gracefully and provide users with helpful messages, rather than showing them raw error information that could expose sensitive details. Rails provides several mechanisms for handling errors in controllers.

1. **Using `rescue_from` to Handle Exceptions**: Rails allows you to use the `rescue_from` method in controllers to catch exceptions and handle them in a central place. For example:

```ruby
class        ApplicationController        <
ActionController::Base
  rescue_from
ActiveRecord::RecordNotFound,        with:
:record_not_found

  private

  def record_not_found
```

```
rer.der     'errors/not_found',    status:
:not_found
  end
end
```

- o This catches any `ActiveRecord::RecordNotFound` exceptions and renders a custom error page with a 404 status.

2. **Handling 404 and 500 Errors**: Rails automatically handles common HTTP errors like `404` (not found) and `500` (internal server error). However, you can customize these pages by creating view templates:

   - o **404 Error**: Create a custom 404 page by adding a `public/404.html` file.
   - o **500 Error**: Create a custom 500 page by adding a `public/500.html` file.

3. **Rendering Custom Error Pages**: If you want to display a custom error message for a specific exception, you can render a custom view in your controller:

```ruby
def show
  @post = Post.find(params[:id])
rescue ActiveRecord::RecordNotFound
  render 'errors/not_found', status: 404
end
```

4. **Handling Validation Errors**: When there are validation errors in a model, Rails automatically adds the errors to the model. You can handle these errors and display them in the view:

ruby

```ruby
def create
  @post = Post.new(post_params)
  if @post.save
    redirect_to @post
  else
    render :new
  end
end
```

In the `new.html.erb` view, you can display the errors like this:

erb

```erb
<% if @post.errors.any? %>
  <ul>
    <% @post.errors.full_messages.each do |message| %>
      <li><%= message %></li>
    <% end %>
  </ul>
<% end %>
```

125

5. **Handling Uncaught Exceptions**: Rails provides a default error handling mechanism for uncaught exceptions, but you can customize the behavior by modifying the config/environments/production.rb file. For instance:

```ruby

config.consider_all_requests_local = false
```

This will show full error reports in development but hide them in production, displaying a friendly error page instead.

Summary

In this chapter, we learned how to handle **errors** and perform **debugging** in Rails applications. We discussed common errors, how to fix them, and how to use the **Rails logger** for debugging. Additionally, we explored strategies for **error handling in controllers**, such as using rescue_from to manage exceptions and provide custom error pages. We also covered using **pry** and the **Rails console** for interactive debugging, and how to gracefully handle user input errors and exceptions to improve the user experience in production environments. With these tools and techniques, you can efficiently debug your application and ensure that errors are handled gracefully for your users.

CHAPTER 12

TESTING IN RAILS

Why Testing is Important: The TDD Approach

Testing is a critical part of software development that ensures your application behaves as expected. It helps identify bugs, provides confidence when making changes, and improves code quality. In Rails, testing is encouraged from the outset to ensure that your app remains stable and maintainable.

Test-Driven Development (TDD) is a methodology that involves writing tests before writing the corresponding code. The TDD approach follows this cycle:

1. **Write a test**: Start by writing a test that defines a feature or a function your application should have.
2. **Run the test**: Initially, this test will fail because the functionality has not yet been implemented.
3. **Write the code**: Implement just enough code to make the test pass.
4. **Refactor**: Once the test passes, refactor the code to ensure it is clean, efficient, and maintainable.
5. **Repeat**: Write the next test and repeat the cycle.

The benefits of TDD include:

- **Higher code quality**: You write tests for every piece of functionality, which ensures that your code works as intended.
- **Fewer bugs**: Since you're constantly running tests, bugs are caught early.
- **Better design**: TDD encourages simpler designs since you write only enough code to pass the tests.
- **Confidence when refactoring**: Having a suite of tests means you can safely make changes and refactor code without worrying about breaking existing functionality.

Rails Testing Framework: Introduction to Minitest

Rails comes with a built-in testing framework called **Minitest**, which provides both unit testing (for models and logic) and integration testing (for controllers and views). Minitest is lightweight, fast, and integrates well with Rails.

1. **Default Testing Setup**: Rails sets up a default testing environment with Minitest. You can run tests using the following command:

```bash

rails test
```

2. **Testing Directories**: By default, Rails creates the following directories for tests:

   o test/models: Contains tests for your models.

   o test/controllers: Contains tests for your controllers.

   o test/integration: Contains tests for end-to-end functionality.

   o test/helpers: Contains tests for your helpers.

   o test/system: Contains tests for user interactions (e.g., clicking buttons, filling forms).

3. **Basic Test Structure**: A basic test file in Rails uses the TestCase class, which inherits from Minitest::Test. Here's an example of a simple test for a Post model:

ruby

```ruby
require 'test_helper'

class PostTest < ActiveSupport::TestCase
  test "should be valid with a title" do
    post = Post.new(title: "Test Post",
content: "Some content.")
    assert post.valid?
  end

  test "should not be valid without a
title" do
```

```
post      =      Post.new(content:      "Some
content.")
    assert_not post.valid?
  end
end
```

- o **assert** is used to check if the condition is true. If it's false, the test fails.
- o **assert_not** is used to check if the condition is false.
- o **valid?** is a built-in ActiveRecord method that checks if the model is valid based on its validations.

Writing Tests for Models, Controllers, and Views

Testing in Rails is typically divided into testing **models**, **controllers**, and **views**. Let's go over how to write tests for each of these components.

1. **Model Tests**: Model tests ensure that your business logic, validations, and associations work as expected.

   Example of a **Post** model test:

   ```ruby
   require 'test_helper'
   ```

131

```
class PostTest < ActiveSupport::TestCase
  test "should not save post without title"
do
    post    =    Post.new(content:    "Some
content.")
    assert_not post.save, "Saved the post
without a title"
  end

  test "should save post with title" do
    post = Post.new(title: "Valid Title",
content: "Some content.")
    assert post.save, "Failed to save the
post with a title"
  end
end
```

This test checks if a `Post` can be saved when it has a title and if it fails when there's no title.

2. **Controller Tests**: Controller tests check whether the controller actions return the correct responses and whether they handle requests correctly.

Example of a **PostsController** test:

```
ruby
```

```
require 'test_helper'

class          PostsControllerTest          <
ActionDispatch::IntegrationTest
  test "should get index" do
    get posts_url
    assert_response :success
  end

  test "should create post" do
    assert_difference('Post.count', 1) do
      post posts_url, params: { post: {
title: 'New Post', content: 'Some content.'
} }
    end
    assert_redirected_to
post_url(Post.last)
  end
end
```

- o   `assert_response :success` checks that the response status is successful (HTTP 200).
- o   `assert_difference` checks if the `Post.count` increased by 1 after the `post` request.
- o   `assert_redirected_to` checks that the user is redirected to the correct URL.

3. **View Tests**: View tests ensure that your templates render correctly, displaying the expected content.

Example of a simple **view test**:

```ruby
require 'test_helper'

class           PostsViewTest        <
ActionDispatch::IntegrationTest
  test "should display post title" do
    post = Post.create(title: "Test Post",
content: "Test content.")
    get post_url(post)
    assert_select 'h1', text: post.title
  end
end
```

- o `assert_select` is used to check that an HTML
  element (`<h1>`) contains the expected text (in this
  case, the `post.title`).

Test-Driven Development: A Complete Example

Now, let's walk through a complete example of Test-Driven
Development (TDD) using Rails. We will create a new feature for
adding comments to posts.

134

1. **Step 1: Write the Test**: Let's start by writing a test for creating a comment on a post. In test/models/comment_test.rb:

```ruby
require 'test_helper'

class CommentTest < ActiveSupport::TestCase
  test "should not save comment without content" do
    comment = Comment.new
    assert_not comment.save, "Saved the comment without content"
  end

  test "should save comment with content" do
    post = posts(:one) # Using a fixture or a factory for posts
    comment = Comment.new(content: "This is a comment.", post: post)
    assert comment.save, "Failed to save the comment"
  end
end
```

2. **Step 2: Run the Test**: Run the test:

135

```bash
bash
```

```bash
rails test
```

The test fails because we haven't written the code for the Comment model yet.

3. **Step 3: Write the Code**: Now we implement the Comment model with a belongs_to :post association and a validates :content, presence: true validation:

```ruby
ruby
```

```ruby
class Comment < ApplicationRecord
  belongs_to :post
  validates :content, presence: true
end
```

4. **Step 4: Run the Test Again**: Now that we've written the code for the Comment model, we can run the test again:

```bash
bash
```

```bash
rails test
```

This time, the test should pass because the validation logic is in place.

5. **Step 5: Refactor (If Necessary)**: If we need to refactor the code, we can do so with confidence, knowing that our tests will alert us if something breaks.

Summary

In this chapter, we discussed the importance of **testing** in Rails applications and the benefits of **Test-Driven Development (TDD)**. We explored the **Minitest** testing framework, which is integrated into Rails by default, and went through how to write tests for **models**, **controllers**, and **views**. We also walked through a complete **TDD example**, where we started with writing tests and then implemented code to make those tests pass, ensuring that our application behaves as expected. TDD not only helps prevent bugs but also encourages writing clean, well-structured, and maintainable code.

CHAPTER 13

BUILDING APIS WITH RUBY ON RAILS

Creating a RESTful API in Rails

A **RESTful API** (Representational State Transfer) is a web service that allows clients to interact with data through HTTP methods like GET, POST, PUT, and DELETE. Rails is well-suited for building APIs due to its support for **RESTful routing** and its powerful **ActiveRecord** ORM.

In Rails, a RESTful API typically exposes resources, and each resource corresponds to a controller and a set of actions (e.g., `index`, `show`, `create`, `update`, `destroy`). Each action corresponds to a CRUD operation for the resource.

Here's how to create a simple RESTful API for managing `Post` resources:

1. **Generate the API Controller**: In Rails, controllers for APIs are often placed in the `app/controllers/api` namespace. To generate an API controller for `Post` resources, you can run:

138

```bash
rails generate controller api/posts
```

2. **Define the API Actions**: In the `Api::PostsController`, define actions for retrieving and manipulating posts. Here's an example of a basic API controller:

```ruby
class Api::PostsController < ApplicationController
  # GET /api/posts
  def index
    @posts = Post.all
    render json: @posts
  end

  # GET /api/posts/:id
  def show
    @post = Post.find_by(id: params[:id])
    if @post
      render json: @post
    else
      render json: { error: 'Post not found' }, status: 404
    end
  end
```

```ruby
  # POST /api/posts
  def create
    @post = Post.new(post_params)
    if @post.save
      render json: @post, status: :created
    else
      render      json:      {      errors:
@post.errors.full_messages      },      status:
:unprocessable_entity
    end
  end


  # PATCH/PUT /api/posts/:id
  def update
    @post = Post.find_by(id: params[:id])
    if @post && @post.update(post_params)
      render json: @post
    else
      render json: { errors: 'Unable to
update post' }, status: 400
    end
  end


  # DELETE /api/posts/:id
  def destroy
    @post = Post.find_by(id: params[:id])
    if @post && @post.destroy
      head :no_content
```

```
    else
      render json: { error: 'Post not found
or not deleted' }, status: 404
    end
  end


  private


  def post_params
    params.require(:post).permit(:title,
:content)
  end
end
```

- o **index**: Retrieves all posts and returns them as JSON.
- o **show**: Retrieves a single post by ID. If found, it returns the post as JSON; otherwise, it returns a 404 error.
- o **create**: Accepts post data, creates a new post, and returns it as JSON. If validation fails, it returns error messages.
- o **update**: Updates an existing post and returns the updated post as JSON. If the post is not found or update fails, it returns a 400 error.
- o **destroy**: Deletes a post and returns a 204 (no content) status.

3. **Add Routes**: Define routes for the API actions in config/routes.rb. To create routes for posts under the api namespace, add:

```ruby
```

```ruby
namespace :api do
  resources :posts
end
```

This will automatically create RESTful routes like /api/posts, /api/posts/:id, etc.

API-only Mode: Understanding and Using Rails for API Development

Rails offers an **API-only mode** that is optimized for building APIs without the overhead of views and other web-specific components. API-only mode reduces unnecessary complexity, providing a lightweight environment focused solely on serving data in formats like JSON.

1. **Setting Up API-only Mode**: To create a new Rails API-only application, use the --api flag when generating a new project:

```bash
```

```
rails new my_api_app --api
```

This generates a Rails app configured to serve APIs, excluding unnecessary middleware for handling views (e.g., ActionView).

2. **Key Differences in API-only Mode**:
   - **No Views**: Since the app is designed to serve data instead of rendering HTML views, Rails disables view-related features.
   - **Middleware**: Rails automatically removes middleware that is unnecessary for API development, such as ActionDispatch::Flash, which is used for flash messages in web apps.
   - **Response Format**: By default, responses are in JSON format. Rails API-only apps also automatically respond with JSON, unless specified otherwise.

3. **Configuring API-only Apps**:
   - You can configure the default response format for all controllers in your ApplicationController:

   ```ruby
   ```

```
class    ApplicationController    <
ActionController::API
  before_action
:set_default_response_format

  private

  def set_default_response_format
    request.format = :json
  end
end
```

4. **Running the API**:

   o   Run the server as usual:

```bash

rails server
```

   o   Your app is now optimized to respond to API requests with JSON data, handling HTTP methods like GET, POST, PUT, and DELETE.

144

Handling JSON Responses: Sending and Receiving Data in JSON Format

When building an API, data is typically sent and received in **JSON** format. Rails provides several built-in tools for working with JSON, both for sending and receiving data from the client.

1. **Sending JSON Responses**: Rails automatically converts Ruby objects to JSON format when you use the `render` method with the `json` option. For example:

   ```ruby
   render json: @post
   ```

   o Rails will convert the `@post` object into a JSON response, using the `as_json` method of the object, which by default includes all model attributes.

2. **Customizing JSON Responses**: You can customize how the data is rendered by using the `as_json` method or creating custom serializers. For example, to include only specific fields in the response:

   ```ruby
   render json: @post.as_json(only: [:id, :title, :content])
   ```

Or use **ActiveModel::Serializer** for more complex serialization:

ruby

```
class              PostSerializer              <
ActiveModel::Serializer
  attributes :id, :title, :content
end
```

- o You can install the gem by adding it to your Gemfile:

  ruby

  ```
  gem 'active_model_serializers'
  ```

- o Then, use it in the controller:

  ruby

  ```
  render json: @post, serializer:
  PostSerializer
  ```

3. **Receiving JSON Data**: To handle incoming JSON data, Rails automatically parses the request body into the params object. For example, when a client sends a POST request with JSON data:

json

```
{
  "title": "New Post",
  "content": "This is a new post."
}
```

Rails will automatically parse this and make the data available via `params[:title]` and `params[:content]`.

In your controller, you would typically write something like this to handle incoming POST data:

ruby

```ruby
def create
  @post = Post.new(post_params)
  if @post.save
    render json: @post, status: :created
  else
    render json: { errors: @post.errors.full_messages }, status: :unprocessable_entity
  end
end

private

def post_params
```

147

```
params.require(:post).permit(:title,
:content)
end
```

Here, `params.require(:post).permit(:title,
:content)` ensures that only `title` and `content` attributes are allowed to be passed to the model.

4. **Handling Errors in JSON**: If an error occurs (e.g., validation failure), you can respond with a JSON error message. For example, if a required parameter is missing:

ruby

```
render json: { error: "Title can't be
blank" }, status: :unprocessable_entity
```

5. **Content Negotiation**: By default, Rails responds with JSON, but you can change this behavior to support other formats, such as XML. You can specify the format in the request:

ruby

```
def create
  respond_to do |format|
    format.json { render json: @post }
    format.xml { render xml: @post.to_xml
}
```

148

```
      end
   end
```

Summary

In this chapter, we learned how to build a **RESTful API** in Rails. We explored how to create API controllers, set up API-only applications for lightweight, efficient development, and handle JSON responses to send and receive data. Rails provides powerful tools for working with APIs, including automatic JSON rendering, request parsing, and customization of response formats. By following RESTful principles and using Rails' built-in features for API development, you can efficiently build scalable, well-structured APIs for your applications.

CHAPTER 14

OPTIMIZING PERFORMANCE IN RAILS

Database Optimization: Efficient Queries with ActiveRecord

Optimizing the performance of your Rails application often involves making your database queries more efficient. Rails uses **ActiveRecord**, which abstracts SQL queries, but it's still important to write efficient queries to minimize the impact on application performance.

Here are some key strategies for optimizing database queries:

1. **Using `select` to Retrieve Only Required Columns**: By default, ActiveRecord retrieves all columns of a record. This can be inefficient if you only need a subset of columns. You can use `select` to specify which columns you want to retrieve:

```ruby
posts              =              Post.select(:id,
:title).where(published: true)
```

This will fetch only the `id` and `title` columns for posts that are marked as `published`, reducing the amount of data loaded into memory.

2. **Using `pluck` to Extract Data**: If you need to retrieve a single column from multiple records, use `pluck`, which is more efficient than loading entire records:

ruby

```
post_titles    =    Post.where(published:
true).pluck(:title)
```

This query will return an array of titles, without loading any other columns from the `posts` table.

3. **Adding Indexes**: Indexes improve the speed of database queries by allowing the database to quickly locate records based on specific columns. You can add indexes in Rails migrations:

ruby

```
add_index :posts, :title
```

Indexes are especially helpful for columns that are frequently queried or used in joins.

4. **Using `find_by` Instead of `find`**: When searching for records by unique attributes (e.g., `id` or `email`), it's better to use `find_by` instead of `find`, as `find_by` doesn't raise an exception if the record is not found:

```ruby
ruby

post = Post.find_by(title: 'My Post')
```

This avoids an exception and improves performance when you don't expect the record to always exist.

5. **Optimizing `where` Clauses**: When applying conditions in the `where` clause, avoid unnecessary operations in the query that could slow it down. For instance:

```ruby
ruby

posts   =   Post.where('created_at   >   ?',
1.week.ago)
```

This query will use a parameterized query to efficiently retrieve posts created in the last week.

6. **Using `find_each` for Large Datasets**: When processing a large number of records, loading them all at once can cause memory bloat. Instead, use `find_each` to iterate over records in batches:

152

```ruby
ruby

Post.find_each(batch_size: 100) do |post|
  # Process each post
end
```

This will fetch records in batches of 100, which is much more memory efficient.

Caching Strategies: How to Use Caching to Speed Up Your App

Caching is one of the most effective ways to improve the performance of your Rails application, especially for frequently accessed data that doesn't change often. Rails offers several caching strategies to reduce the number of requests to the database and speed up response times.

1. **Fragment Caching**: Fragment caching allows you to cache parts of a view that don't change often. For example, you might cache the sidebar of a page that displays user statistics, which doesn't change frequently:

```erb
erb

<% cache('user_sidebar') do %>
  <div class="sidebar">
    <%= render 'user_stats' %>
  </div>
```

```
<% end %>
```

This will cache the rendered HTML of the `user_stats` partial and reuse it on subsequent requests until the cache expires or is invalidated.

2. **Action Caching**: Action caching caches the entire output of a controller action. This can be useful if the entire page doesn't change frequently. However, action caching has been deprecated in Rails 5 and is replaced with **controller caching**:

```ruby
ruby
```

```ruby
class           PostsController          <
ApplicationController
  caches_action :index
end
```

This will cache the response of the `index` action and serve the cached version until the cache is cleared or expires.

3. **Low-Level Caching**: Rails supports low-level caching with `Rails.cache`, which allows you to store arbitrary data in the cache. This can be used for caching database queries or computationally expensive operations:

```ruby
ruby
```

```ruby
@posts = Rails.cache.fetch('recent_posts')
do
  Post.recent.limit(5)
end
```

This stores the result of the `Post.recent.limit(5)` query in the cache, and future requests will use the cached result.

4. **Russian Doll Caching**: Russian doll caching is an advanced caching strategy that caches nested fragments. This allows you to cache parts of a page, including nested partials, and update only the parts that change.

erb

```erb
<%= cache([post, post.updated_at]) do %>
  <div class="post">
    <%= render post %>
  </div>
<% end %>
```

In this example, the cache key is based on both the post object and its `updated_at` timestamp. This ensures that if the post is updated, the cache will expire and the page will be regenerated.

155

5. **Expire Caches**: Cache expiration is crucial for ensuring that your cached content doesn't become stale. You can manually expire a cache by using the `expire_fragment` or `expire_action` methods:

```ruby
expire_fragment('user_sidebar')
```

This will expire the cached `user_sidebar` fragment, forcing it to be regenerated the next time it is requested.

6. **Caching in Production**: In production, you typically use a caching store like **Memcached** or **Redis** for storing cached data. To configure this in Rails, modify `config/environments/production.rb`:

```ruby
config.cache_store = :mem_cache_store
```

This will store your cached data in a Memcached server.

Eager Loading vs Lazy Loading: Best Practices for Fetching Data

When dealing with associations in Rails, **eager loading** and **lazy loading** are two strategies for loading related records. Choosing the right approach can greatly affect your application's performance.

1. **Lazy Loading (Default Behavior)**: Lazy loading means that associated records are fetched only when they are accessed. For example, if you have a `Post` with many `Comments`, and you access the comments later in the code:

    ```ruby
    post = Post.find(1)
    comments = post.comments
    ```

    The comments are not loaded until `post.comments` is accessed. This can result in **N+1 query problems**, where each post's comments are fetched individually, leading to multiple database queries.

    Problem Example:

    ```ruby
    posts = Post.all
    posts.each do |post|
      puts post.comments.count
    end
    ```

157

This will execute an additional query for each post, leading to N+1 queries.

2. **Eager Loading**: Eager loading loads associated records as part of the initial query to avoid N+1 queries. In Rails, you can use the `includes` method to eager load associations:

ruby

```
posts = Post.includes(:comments).all
posts.each do |post|
  puts post.comments.count
end
```

In this case, Rails will use a **single SQL query** to fetch all posts and their associated comments, avoiding N+1 queries.

3. **Eager Loading with `joins`**: If you want to filter or sort data based on associated records, you can use `joins` with eager loading. This allows you to perform operations like filtering posts that have comments:

ruby

```
posts                                   =
Post.joins(:comments).where('comments.cre
ated_at > ?', 1.week.ago)
```

This will perform a single SQL query that joins the `posts` and `comments` tables, applying the filter condition.

4. **When to Use Eager Loading**: Eager loading is recommended when you know you will need to access an association for multiple records in a loop, as it minimizes database queries. It's particularly useful for **index actions** where you might list multiple records along with their associated data.

5. **When to Use Lazy Loading**: Lazy loading is suitable when you only need to access an association occasionally or for a small number of records. It's also useful when you want to minimize the amount of data loaded into memory.

Summary

In this chapter, we explored several techniques for **optimizing performance** in Rails. We discussed how to optimize **database queries** using ActiveRecord, including using `select`, `pluck`, and adding indexes. We also covered **caching strategies** such as fragment caching, action caching, and low-level caching to improve application speed by reducing database queries. Additionally, we examined the difference between **eager loading** and **lazy loading**, highlighting best practices for fetching related data to avoid N+1 query problems and improve performance. By implementing these strategies, you can ensure that your Rails application is efficient, scalable, and performs well even as your user base grows.

CHAPTER 15

BACKGROUND JOBS AND ASYNCHRONOUS PROCESSING

Introduction to Background Jobs in Rails

In Rails, **background jobs** are used to perform tasks asynchronously, allowing long-running processes to be handled outside the main request-response cycle. This ensures that the user doesn't have to wait for resource-intensive tasks (like sending emails, processing images, or interacting with external APIs) to complete before receiving a response. Background jobs help improve performance, provide a better user experience, and allow your application to scale more efficiently.

For example, in an application where you want to send an email after a user registers, instead of sending the email during the registration process, you can offload this task to a background job. This way, the user can complete their registration without delay while the email is sent in the background.

Rails provides several tools and libraries for handling background jobs, with **Sidekiq** being one of the most popular and powerful solutions.

Using Sidekiq for Asynchronous Jobs

Sidekiq is a highly efficient background job processing library for Ruby and Rails. It runs jobs asynchronously in separate threads, allowing you to process jobs concurrently. Sidekiq is particularly known for its speed, scalability, and ability to process jobs in parallel using multiple threads.

1. **Installing Sidekiq**: To begin using Sidekiq in a Rails application, you need to install the `sidekiq` gem. Add it to your Gemfile:

```ruby
gem 'sidekiq'
```

Then, run `bundle install` to install the gem:

```bash
bundle install
```

2. **Setting Up Redis**: Sidekiq uses **Redis** as its backend to store job data. You need to have Redis installed and running on your machine or use a cloud-based Redis provider like Redis Labs or Amazon ElastiCache.

To install Redis on your local machine, you can follow the instructions from the official Redis website. For production, you'll need to configure your application to connect to a Redis server.

3. **Configuring Sidekiq in Rails**: After installing the gem and setting up Redis, you need to configure Sidekiq in your Rails application. You can create a new initializer file in `config/initializers/sidekiq.rb`:

```ruby
Sidekiq.configure_server do |config|
  config.redis = { url:
'redis://localhost:6379/0', namespace:
'myapp_production' }
end

Sidekiq.configure_client do |config|
  config.redis = { url:
'redis://localhost:6379/0', namespace:
'myapp_production' }
end
```

This configuration tells Sidekiq where to find Redis and sets a namespace for your application's data.

4. **Creating a Background Job**: To create a background job, use the `sidekiq:job` generator:

```bash
bash
```

```bash
rails          generate          sidekiq:job
send_welcome_email
```

This generates a new job file in `app/jobs/send_welcome_email_job.rb`:

```ruby
ruby
```

```ruby
class SendWelcomeEmailJob
  include Sidekiq::Job

  def perform(user_id)
    user = User.find(user_id)

UserMailer.welcome_email(user).deliver_no
w
  end
end
```

In this example, the `SendWelcomeEmailJob` is a background job that sends a welcome email to a user. The `perform` method takes a `user_id` as an argument, finds the user in the database, and sends the email asynchronously.

5. **Enqueuing Jobs**: To enqueue a job, you use the `perform_async` method provided by Sidekiq. For

example, to enqueue the `SendWelcomeEmailJob` in a controller or service:

```ruby

SendWelcomeEmailJob.perform_async(user.id
)
```

This adds the job to the Sidekiq queue, and it will be processed in the background by a Sidekiq worker.

Setting Up and Managing Background Jobs

1. **Running Sidekiq**: To start processing background jobs, you need to start the Sidekiq worker. In your terminal, run the following command:

```bash

bundle exec sidekiq
```

This will start a Sidekiq worker that listens for incoming jobs and processes them.

2. **Web Interface for Monitoring**: Sidekiq provides a web-based monitoring interface that allows you to track job status, retries, and failures. To enable it, add the following to your `config/routes.rb`:

```ruby
require 'sidekiq/web'
Rails.application.routes.draw do
  mount Sidekiq::Web => '/sidekiq'
end
```

Now, you can visit `/sidekiq` in your browser (e.g., `http://localhost:3000/sidekiq`) to monitor and manage your background jobs.

3. **Retrying Failed Jobs**: By default, Sidekiq will automatically retry failed jobs. You can configure the retry behavior in the job itself:

```ruby
class SendWelcomeEmailJob
  include Sidekiq::Job

  sidekiq_options retry: 5  # Retry the job up to 5 times

  def perform(user_id)
    # Job logic
  end
end
```

166

This specifies that the job should be retried up to 5 times before giving up. You can also configure custom retry logic using a `sidekiq_options` block.

4. **Job Scheduling**: Sidekiq also allows you to schedule jobs to run at a specific time or after a delay. For example:

```ruby
SendWelcomeEmailJob.perform_in(5.minutes,
user.id)  # Run after 5 minutes
SendWelcomeEmailJob.perform_at(Time.now  +
1.day, user.id)  # Run at a specific time
```

These methods allow you to schedule jobs for future execution, rather than running them immediately.

Best Practices for Handling Background Tasks

1. **Keep Jobs Small and Focused**: Each background job should perform a single, well-defined task. Avoid writing complex jobs that perform multiple tasks in one go. Breaking jobs down into smaller, focused tasks makes them easier to manage, monitor, and retry if necessary.

Example:

    o   Instead of sending a welcome email, updating user data, and generating a PDF all in one job, split them into separate jobs: one for email, one for data update, and one for PDF generation.

2. **Handle Errors Gracefully**: Always handle potential errors within your jobs. Sidekiq provides automatic retries, but it's still important to anticipate failure scenarios. For example, if the email service is down, catch the error and log it:

```ruby
begin

UserMailer.welcome_email(user).deliver_no
w
rescue => e
  Sidekiq.logger.error  "Failed  to  send
email: #{e.message}"
  raise e
end
```

3. **Avoid Blocking the Main Thread**: Background jobs are meant to run in the background, so avoid long-running, blocking operations. If a job depends on an external API, consider using retries with exponential backoff or splitting the task into smaller, faster jobs.

4. **Use a Reliable Job Queue**: While Sidekiq uses Redis to manage job queues, it's essential to ensure Redis is configured and scaled properly for your needs. Use **Redis replication** and **persistence** settings to ensure job data is not lost in case of failure.

5. **Monitor and Retry Failed Jobs**: Use Sidekiq's built-in web interface to monitor the success or failure of jobs. You can manually retry failed jobs or examine the logs to determine why a job failed. Implementing a **dead-letter queue** (DLQ) to capture jobs that repeatedly fail can be useful for debugging.

6. **Batching Jobs**: When you need to process a large number of items, use batching to reduce the strain on the system. For example, rather than processing hundreds of items in a single job, you can process them in smaller batches:

```ruby
ruby

User.find_in_batches(batch_size: 100) do
|batch|
  batch.each do |user|

SendWelcomeEmailJob.perform_async(user.id
)
  end
end
```

169

Summary

In this chapter, we covered the essentials of **background job processing** in Rails. We introduced **Sidekiq**, a powerful tool for handling asynchronous tasks, and demonstrated how to set up and manage background jobs in a Rails application. We explored job scheduling, error handling, job retries, and how to use Sidekiq's web interface to monitor job status. We also discussed best practices for creating efficient background tasks, such as keeping jobs small, handling errors, and monitoring job performance. By using background jobs, you can offload heavy tasks and ensure your application remains responsive, scalable, and efficient.

CHAPTER 16

WEBSOCKETS AND REAL-TIME FEATURES

What Are WebSockets?: Enabling Real-Time Communication

WebSockets is a protocol that enables full-duplex, real-time communication between a client (such as a web browser) and a server. Unlike traditional HTTP requests, where the client makes a request and waits for a response, WebSockets allow the server and client to send messages to each other at any time without waiting for a request. This makes it ideal for applications that require real-time updates, such as messaging apps, live notifications, or collaborative tools.

Here's how WebSockets differ from regular HTTP:

- **HTTP**: A client makes a request, and the server responds. Communication is one-way (request-response).
- **WebSockets**: The connection is established once, and both the client and server can send messages to each other at any time during the connection.

In Rails, **ActionCable** provides an easy-to-use framework for implementing WebSockets in your application. ActionCable integrates WebSockets seamlessly with the rest of the Rails framework, enabling you to build real-time features like live updates, notifications, or chat systems.

Implementing Real-Time Features with ActionCable

ActionCable is the Rails framework for handling WebSockets. It allows you to integrate real-time features into your application with minimal setup.

1. **Setting Up ActionCable**: To use ActionCable in your Rails application, follow these steps:
   - **Ensure Redis is installed**: ActionCable requires **Redis** as a pub/sub (publish/subscribe) system for broadcasting messages. Install Redis on your system or use a cloud provider for Redis.

     You can install Redis locally via Homebrew on macOS:

     ```bash
     brew install redis
     ```

     Or on Ubuntu:

```bash
bash

sudo apt-get install redis-server
```

- o **Configure Redis in `cable.yml`**: In the `config/cable.yml` file, configure ActionCable to use Redis in development and production:

```yaml
yaml

development:
  adapter: redis
  url: redis://localhost:6379/0
  channel_prefix: myapp_development

production:
  adapter: redis
  url: redis://localhost:6379/0
  channel_prefix: myapp_production
  urlparam:        {        "password":
"your_redis_password" }
```

- o **Enable WebSocket Server in `config/environments/development.rb`**:

```ruby
ruby
```

```
config.action_cable.url          =
"ws://localhost:3000/cable"
```

2. **Creating a Channel**: ActionCable uses channels to handle WebSocket communication. A channel is like a controller for WebSockets. Each channel can handle real-time communication for a specific feature, such as chat messages or notifications.

   You can generate a new channel with the Rails generator:

   ```bash
   bash
   ```

   ```
   rails generate channel chat
   ```

   This will generate a channel file (`app/channels/chat_channel.rb`) and a JavaScript file (`app/javascript/channels/chat_channel.js`). The `chat_channel.rb` file defines the logic for handling WebSocket connections, while the JavaScript file manages the frontend WebSocket connection.

3. **Setting Up the Chat Channel (Backend)**: In `app/channels/chat_channel.rb`, define the logic for broadcasting and receiving messages:

   ```ruby
   ruby
   ```

174

```ruby
class          ChatChannel          <
ApplicationCable::Channel
  def subscribed
    stream_from "chat_#{params[:room]}"
  end

  def unsubscribed
    # Any cleanup needed when channel is
unsubscribed
  end

  def send_message(data)

ActionCable.server.broadcast("chat_#{para
ms[:room]}", message: data['message'])
  end
end
```

- o **subscribed**: This method is called when a user connects to the channel. We stream data from a specific chat room (identified by `params[:room]`).
- o **unsubscribed**: This method is called when a user disconnects from the channel.
- o **send_message**: This method is called to broadcast messages to all users in the chat room.

4. **Setting Up the Chat Channel (Frontend)**: In `app/javascript/channels/chat_channel.js`, set

175

up the WebSocket connection and handle sending and receiving messages:

```javascript
import consumer from "./consumer"

consumer.subscriptions.create({ channel: "ChatChannel", room: "general" }, {
  connected() {
    console.log("Connected to the chat room!");
  },

  disconnected() {
    console.log("Disconnected from the chat room!");
  },

  received(data) {
    const message = document.createElement("p");
    message.innerText = data.message;

document.getElementById("messages").appendChild(message);
  },

  sendMessage(message) {
```

```
this.perform('send_message',          {
message: message });
  }
});
```

- o **connected**: This callback is triggered when the WebSocket connection is established.

- o **disconnected**: This callback is triggered when the WebSocket connection is closed.

- o **received**: This callback is triggered when a message is received from the server (e.g., when a new message is broadcast to the chat).

- o **sendMessage**: This method sends messages to the backend when called.

5. **Broadcasting Messages**: In the backend (chat_channel.rb), we broadcast messages to all subscribers using ActionCable.server.broadcast. The message will be broadcast to all clients connected to the specified channel.

Building a Real-Time Chat Application

Now that we have a basic understanding of how to set up ActionCable, let's build a simple **real-time chat application** where users can send messages to each other in real-time.

1. **Create a Chat Model**: To store chat messages in the database, generate a `ChatMessage` model:

bash

```
rails generate model ChatMessage content:string room:string user:references
rails db:migrate
```

This will create a `ChatMessage` model with a `content`, `room`, and `user_id`. The `room` column allows us to support different chat rooms.

2. **Modify the Chat Channel (Backend)**: In `app/channels/chat_channel.rb`, modify the `send_message` method to save the message to the database and then broadcast it to the channel:

ruby

```
class ChatChannel < ApplicationCable::Channel
  def subscribed
    stream_from "chat_#{params[:room]}"
  end

  def unsubscribed
    # Cleanup
  end
```

```ruby
def send_message(data)
  message = ChatMessage.create!(
    content: data['message'],
    room: params[:room],
    user: current_user
  )

ActionCable.server.broadcast("chat_#{params[:room]}", message: message.content)
  end
end
```

- o **ChatMessage.create!**: Saves the chat message to the database.
- o **ActionCable.server.broadcast**: Broadcasts the message to all users in the specified room.

3. **Modify the Chat Channel (Frontend)**: Update the frontend to send and display messages:

```javascript
javascript

import consumer from "./consumer"

const chatRoom = "general"; // Example room

const messagesContainer = document.getElementById("messages");
```

179

```
consumer.subscriptions.create({   channel:
"ChatChannel", room: chatRoom }, {
  connected() {
    console.log("Connected to chat room:",
chatRoom);
  },

  disconnected() {
    console.log("Disconnected   from   chat
room:", chatRoom);
  },

  received(data) {
    const             message             =
document.createElement("p");
    message.innerText = data.message;

messagesContainer.appendChild(message);
  },

  sendMessage(message) {
    this.perform('send_message',            {
message: message });
  }
});

document.getElementById("send_button").ad
dEventListener("click", () => {
```

```
const            messageInput            =
document.getElementById("message_input");
  const message = messageInput.value;


consumer.subscriptions.subscriptions[0].s
endMessage(message);
  messageInput.value = "";
});
```

4. **Create the Chat View**: In the chat view
   (app/views/chats/show.html.erb), add the
   following HTML to display messages and input a new
   message:

   erb

```erb
<div id="messages"></div>


<textarea                id="message_input"
placeholder="Type                      your
message"></textarea>
<button id="send_button">Send</button>
```

5. **Testing the Chat Application**: Run your Rails server,
   navigate to the chat view, and you'll be able to send
   messages that are instantly broadcast to all connected
   users in the same chat room.

181

Summary

In this chapter, we covered the basics of **WebSockets** and how to implement **real-time features** in Rails using **ActionCable**. We learned how to set up WebSocket connections, create channels for real-time communication, and broadcast messages between clients. Then, we built a simple **real-time chat application** that allows users to send and receive messages instantly. ActionCable provides a robust and easy-to-use way to integrate WebSockets into a Rails application, enabling real-time interactivity and improving user engagement.

CHAPTER 17

FRONT-END INTEGRATION WITH RAILS

Working with JavaScript and Rails: Integration Strategies

Integrating JavaScript with Rails allows you to enhance the interactivity and dynamic behavior of your web application. Rails provides several strategies for integrating JavaScript into the app, ranging from simple inline scripts to complex front-end frameworks. Understanding the best ways to incorporate JavaScript into your Rails application is crucial for building responsive, modern applications.

Rails provides multiple ways to integrate JavaScript:

1. **The Asset Pipeline**: The **Asset Pipeline** allows you to organize, manage, and compress your JavaScript files. Rails uses Sprockets (or Webpacker in later versions) to handle asset management. You can add JavaScript directly to the application by placing it in the `app/assets/javascripts` directory.

For example, a simple JavaScript file (`app/assets/javascripts/application.js`) might look like:

```javascript
```

```javascript
console.log("Welcome to Rails!");
```

2. **Using Webpacker**: **Webpacker** is the default solution for handling JavaScript in Rails (starting from Rails 6). Webpacker provides more flexibility and power by allowing you to integrate modern JavaScript tools and frameworks (like React or Vue) with ease.

   You can configure Webpacker by running:

```bash
```

```bash
rails webpacker:install
```

   After installation, JavaScript code is typically placed in the `app/javascript` directory, where Webpacker can compile it. For example, you can create React or Vue components here.

3. **Turbolinks**: **Turbolinks** is a JavaScript library built into Rails that speeds up page navigation by loading only the body and merging it into the current page instead of reloading the entire page. While it's a powerful feature, it

requires careful integration with JavaScript to avoid issues with event listeners.

If you are using modern front-end libraries, you might disable Turbolinks and use React or Vue for full front-end rendering.

4. **StimulusJS and UJS (Unobtrusive JavaScript)**: Rails comes with **StimulusJS** (a minimal JavaScript framework) and **UJS** to make working with JavaScript simpler. Stimulus allows you to use JavaScript for small dynamic behaviors without fully adopting a complex front-end framework.

Using Rails with React or Vue: Front-End Frameworks in Rails Apps

React and Vue are two of the most popular JavaScript frameworks for building modern user interfaces. Both integrate well with Rails, allowing you to use them for building dynamic front-end components while Rails manages the back-end.

1. **Using React with Rails**: React is a JavaScript library for building user interfaces, particularly single-page applications (SPAs). Integrating React with Rails is simple when using **Webpacker**, which is the default for managing JavaScript in Rails.

Steps for Integrating React:

- Install Webpacker and React:

```bash
rails webpacker:install
rails webpacker:install:react
```

- Create a React component in the app/javascript/components directory:

```javascript
// app/javascript/components/HelloWorld.jsx
import React from "react";

const HelloWorld = ({ name }) => {
  return <h1>Hello, {name}!</h1>;
};

export default HelloWorld;
```

- Use the React component in your Rails view:

```erb
```

```
<!-- app/views/posts/index.html.erb
-->
<div id="hello-react"></div>
<%=             javascript_pack_tag
'hello_react' %>
```

○   Render the React component inside the HTML:

```
javascript

//
app/javascript/packs/hello_react.js
import React from "react";
import ReactDOM from "react-dom";
import       HelloWorld       from
"components/HelloWorld";

document.addEventListener("DOMConte
ntLoaded", () => {
  ReactDOM.render(<HelloWorld
name="Rails"                 />,
document.getElementById("hello-
react"));
});
```

React components can now be used in your Rails views. React is great for building complex, interactive UIs, and Rails serves as the back-end to handle database interactions, authentication, etc.

2. **Using Vue with Rails**: Vue.js is another popular JavaScript framework that is easy to integrate into a Rails app, and it's known for its simplicity and flexibility.

Steps for Integrating Vue:

o Install Webpacker and Vue:

```bash
rails webpacker:install
rails webpacker:install:vue
```

o Create a Vue component:

```javascript
// app/javascript/components/HelloWorld.vue
<template>
  <div>
    <h1>Hello, {{ name }}!</h1>
  </div>
</template>

<script>
export default {
  props: ['name']
}
```

188

```
</script>
```

o   Use the Vue component in your Rails view:

erb

```
<!-- app/views/posts/index.html.erb
-->
<div id="hello-vue"></div>
<%= javascript_pack_tag 'hello_vue'
%>
```

o   Render the Vue component inside the HTML:

javascript

```
// app/javascript/packs/hello_vue.js
import Vue from 'vue'
import        HelloWorld        from
'components/HelloWorld.vue'

document.addEventListener('DOMConte
ntLoaded', () => {
  const app = new Vue({
    el: '#hello-vue',
    render:  h  =>  h(HelloWorld,  {
props: { name: 'Rails' } })
  })
})
```

Vue.js provides an elegant way to build single-page applications with a minimal learning curve. It can handle interactive UIs while Rails continues to manage the server-side logic.

StimulusJS: Enhancing Your Rails App with Minimal JavaScript

StimulusJS is a modest JavaScript framework that complements traditional server-rendered applications. It was designed to provide just enough interactivity for your Rails app without requiring a heavy front-end framework like React or Vue. Stimulus works by enhancing HTML with **data attributes** that connect HTML elements to JavaScript controllers.

1. **Setting Up Stimulus**: Stimulus comes preconfigured with Rails 6+ in the `app/javascript/controllers` directory. If you need to install it, run:

```bash

rails webpacker:install:stimulus
```

2. **Creating a Stimulus Controller**: Stimulus controllers are used to handle interactions with elements in your views. For example, let's create a `hello_controller.js` that changes the text content when a button is clicked:

190

- **app/javascript/controllers/hello_controller.js**:

javascript

```javascript
import { Controller } from "stimulus";

export default class extends Controller {
  static targets = ["output"];

  greet() {
    this.outputTarget.textContent = "Hello, Stimulus!";
  }
}
```

- **app/views/posts/index.html.erb**:

erb

```erb
<div data-controller="hello">
  <button data-action="click->hello#greet">Greet</button>
  <p data-hello-target="output">Hello, World!</p>
</div>
```

191

3. In this example, when the button is clicked, the `greet` method is triggered, updating the `<p>` element with the message "Hello, Stimulus!"

4. **Using Stimulus for Simple Interactions**: Stimulus is perfect for adding simple interactivity like toggling visibility, showing or hiding elements, or submitting forms without reloading the page. It allows you to avoid the complexity of full front-end frameworks for small interactions.

5. **Stimulus with Turbolinks**: Stimulus works well with **Turbolinks** (which speeds up page navigation by only updating the body and merging it with the current page). If you're using Turbolinks, Stimulus controllers will automatically reinitialize when the page is replaced.

Summary

In this chapter, we explored different strategies for **integrating front-end technologies** with Rails, including how to work with JavaScript, and how to incorporate front-end frameworks like **React** and **Vue**. We also introduced **StimulusJS**, a minimalistic framework that enhances your Rails app with just the right amount of interactivity. Using **React** or **Vue** with Rails is ideal for more complex, interactive user interfaces, while **Stimulus** is perfect for simpler, server-rendered applications that don't require heavy

JavaScript frameworks. By leveraging the power of Rails alongside these front-end tools, you can build dynamic, modern applications that provide a smooth user experience without sacrificing the simplicity and efficiency of Rails.

CHAPTER 18

ASSET PIPELINE AND MANAGING STATIC FILES

What is the Asset Pipeline?

The **Asset Pipeline** is a feature in Rails that provides a framework for handling and optimizing static files, such as JavaScript, CSS, and images. It is responsible for combining, minifying, and serving these assets efficiently to improve performance. The Asset Pipeline is especially useful for managing complex assets, reducing file size, and ensuring your application runs smoothly in production.

The Asset Pipeline works by taking all your JavaScript, CSS, and image files, processing them, and generating optimized versions that are ready for deployment. It also allows for organizing and structuring your assets in a way that simplifies management and integration into your Rails application.

Key features of the Asset Pipeline include:

- **Preprocessing**: The Asset Pipeline allows you to preprocess files written in languages like **Sass**,

194

CoffeeScript, and **ES6**. It compiles them into standard CSS, JavaScript, and other formats.

- **Concatenation**: It combines multiple files into a single file to reduce the number of HTTP requests made by the browser.

- **Minification**: The Asset Pipeline minimizes the size of assets by removing unnecessary whitespace, comments, and shortening variable names.

In Rails 6+, the Asset Pipeline is handled by **Sprockets** and **Webpacker** (for more modern JavaScript features).

Managing JavaScript, CSS, and Images in Rails

Rails provides a systematic way to manage static assets like **JavaScript**, **CSS**, and **images**. Let's explore how each of these types of assets is managed in Rails.

1. **Managing JavaScript**: JavaScript files in Rails are typically placed in the `app/assets/javascripts` directory. Rails provides support for writing modular JavaScript by allowing you to structure files in subdirectories. For example:
   - `app/assets/javascripts/application.js`: This is the main JavaScript file for your app, and it is automatically included in all pages.

195

o `app/assets/javascripts/foo.js`: This file can contain JavaScript specific to a certain feature or page.

The `application.js` file should use the `//= require` directive to include other JavaScript files:

```javascript
//= require jquery
//= require bootstrap
//= require_tree .
```

- o **`//= require jquery`**: This includes the jQuery library.
- o **`//= require bootstrap`**: This includes the Bootstrap framework.
- o **`//= require_tree .`**: This includes all JavaScript files in the current directory and subdirectories.

Rails also supports **ES6 modules** when using **Webpacker**, so you can use modern JavaScript syntax, including `import` and `export`.

2. **Managing CSS**: Rails uses **Sass** by default for handling CSS, which provides powerful features like variables, nesting, and mixins. CSS files are placed in the

196

`app/assets/stylesheets` directory. Similar to JavaScript files, you can organize your styles into smaller, modular files.

For example:

- o `app/assets/stylesheets/application.css.scss`: The main CSS file where all styles are included.
- o `app/assets/stylesheets/foo.scss`: A specific stylesheet for a particular feature.

In the `application.css.scss` file, you would include other stylesheets using `@import`:

scss

```
@import "bootstrap";
@import "custom";
@import "fonts";
```

Sass allows you to use more advanced CSS features like variables:

scss

```
$primary-color: #333;

body {
```

```
color: $primary-color;
}
```

If you want to add custom CSS for specific pages, you can create separate style files and include them only for the corresponding views or layouts.

3. **Managing Images**: Images in Rails are typically stored in the `app/assets/images` directory. You can include images in your stylesheets or views using the **image_tag** helper or **asset_path**.

   o   In a view, you can use the `image_tag` helper to display an image:

   ```erb
   <%= image_tag "logo.png" %>
   ```

   o   In CSS, you can reference images using the `asset-path` helper:

   ```scss
   background-image:           image-url("background.png");
   ```

4. Rails automatically handles image assets, allowing you to reference them with their paths while automatically managing caching and versioning.

5. **Using Webpacker for Modern JavaScript**: For modern JavaScript features such as React, Vue, or Angular, Rails uses **Webpacker**. It allows you to manage JavaScript with modern tools like Babel, Webpack, and Yarn. You can install Webpacker with the following command:

```bash
bash
```

```bash
rails webpacker:install
```

This sets up a new directory (`app/javascript`) for managing JavaScript assets. You can use `import` and `export` to manage modules, and integrate JavaScript frameworks like React, Vue, or others.

Minification and Compression: How Rails Handles Assets for Performance

Minification and compression are essential for optimizing the performance of your Rails application, especially in production. These processes reduce the size of assets (JavaScript, CSS, images) to decrease load times and improve the overall user experience.

1. **Minification**: Minification is the process of removing unnecessary characters (such as whitespace, comments,

and line breaks) from JavaScript and CSS files without changing the functionality of the code.

In Rails, minification is handled automatically in the production environment. When you run `rails assets:precompile`, Rails will minify and compress your assets, making them smaller and faster to load.

- o For JavaScript, Rails uses **Uglifier** (by default) to minify the code.
- o For CSS, Rails uses **Sass** for CSS compression and minification.
- o For HTML, Rails uses **HTMLCompressor** to compress HTML output.

You can specify custom minification settings in `config/environments/production.rb` if needed:

```ruby
config.assets.js_compressor = :uglifier
config.assets.css_compressor = :sass
```

2. **Compression**: Compression further reduces asset sizes by applying algorithms (like Gzip or Brotli) to compress files. In production, Rails automatically serves compressed assets to users when they are available. This

reduces the bandwidth required to transfer the files to users.

- o In your config/environments/production.rb, ensure that compression is enabled:

```ruby
config.assets.js_compressor = :uglifier
config.assets.css_compressor = :sass
config.assets.compile = false
config.assets.digest = true
config.public_file_server.headers = {
    'Cache-Control' => "public, max-age=#{1.year.to_i}"
}
```

3. **Asset Versioning**: Rails uses a technique called **fingerprinting** to manage cacheable assets efficiently. This involves adding a unique hash to the filenames of assets (like application-123abc.js). This hash changes whenever the file is modified, which prevents browsers from caching outdated files.

- o For example, application.css may become application-123abc.css after it is compiled.

201

- o This helps ensure that when assets change, users always receive the updated version rather than using a cached file.

4. **Precompiling Assets**: When deploying a Rails app to production, you typically need to precompile your assets. This is done by running:

```bash

rails assets:precompile
```

This command compiles all your JavaScript, CSS, and image files and places them in the `public/assets` directory, ready to be served to users.

Summary

In this chapter, we explored the **Asset Pipeline** in Rails, which allows you to manage and optimize static files such as JavaScript, CSS, and images. We discussed how to handle assets in Rails, including organizing and referencing files using the **Asset Pipeline** and **Webpacker** for modern JavaScript frameworks. We also covered **minification** and **compression** strategies for improving performance, including automatic minification of JavaScript and CSS, and how asset versioning and compression help reduce file sizes and improve load times. By using these tools and techniques, you can ensure that your Rails application is both fast and efficient, providing a smooth experience for users.

CHAPTER 19

DEPLOYING RAILS APPLICATIONS

Preparing Your App for Production: Configuration Tips

Before deploying your Rails application to a production environment, it's important to ensure that it is configured correctly to handle the demands of live traffic. Production configurations optimize performance, security, and scalability.

1. **Environment Configuration**: Rails provides different configuration settings for each environment (development, test, production). In the production environment, you need to adjust several settings for security and performance.

   o **Database Configuration**: In config/database.yml, ensure that your production database is properly set up. You might use PostgreSQL, MySQL, or another database service. A typical configuration for PostgreSQL in production would look like this:

   yaml

```
production:
  adapter: postgresql
  encoding: unicode
  database: myapp_production
  pool: 5
  username: myapp_user
  password:                    <%=
ENV['DATABASE_PASSWORD'] %>
```

Use environment variables (ENV) for sensitive information such as passwords.

o **Secrets and Credentials**: Ensure that sensitive information, such as API keys and credentials, is securely stored. Rails uses **Credentials** (config/credentials.yml.enc) for managing secret data. You can edit it using:

```bash
```

```
rails credentials:edit
```

This will allow you to add credentials that are securely encrypted.

o **Precompiling Assets**: Rails needs to precompile assets for production to improve load times. In the production environment, set

205

```
config.assets.compile    =    false    in
config/environments/production.rb   to
```
avoid dynamically compiling assets at runtime.
Precompile assets before deploying:

```
bash
```

```
rails assets:precompile
```

o **Cache Store**: In production, it's important to set up caching for better performance. You can use a memory store, file store, or cloud-based cache like Redis:

```
ruby
```

```
config.cache_store            =
:mem_cache_store, "localhost"
```

o **Logging**: By default, Rails logs at the `debug` level, which is too verbose for production. Change the log level to `info` in config/environments/production.rb:

```
ruby
```

```
config.log_level = :info
```

o **Error Reporting**: In production, you want to show users friendly error pages without exposing sensitive details. Ensure that `config.consider_all_requests_local` is set to `false`:

```ruby
ruby
```

```ruby
config.consider_all_requests_local =
false
```

o **Database Migrations**: Run migrations after deploying your app to ensure that your production database is up to date:

```bash
bash
```

```bash
heroku run rake db:migrate
```

o **Security Settings**: Make sure you enable various security features:

```ruby
ruby
```

```ruby
config.force_ssl = true
config.middleware.use Rack::Attack
```

Deploying to Heroku: A Step-by-Step Deployment Guide

Heroku is a cloud platform that simplifies application deployment, making it an excellent choice for deploying Rails apps quickly. Heroku manages most of the infrastructure, so you don't need to worry about servers, databases, or scaling directly.

1. **Creating a Heroku Account**: First, sign up for a free Heroku account at heroku.com.

2. **Installing the Heroku CLI**: Download and install the Heroku CLI to interact with Heroku from your terminal:

```bash

https://devcenter.heroku.com/articles/heroku-cli
```

3. **Preparing Your Rails App**:
    - Ensure your app is using a supported database (e.g., PostgreSQL).
    - Make sure all production dependencies (e.g., Redis for caching, Postgres for the database) are listed in your Gemfile and added via:

```ruby

gem 'pg'
gem 'redis'
```

4. **Setting Up the Heroku App**: Initialize your Git repository (if not already done):

bash

```
git init
git add .
git commit -m "Initial commit"
```

Create a new Heroku application:

bash

```
heroku create my-rails-app
```

This command will:

- o Create a new app on Heroku.
- o Set up a remote Git repository named `heroku`.

5. **Deploying to Heroku**: Push your application to Heroku:

bash

```
git push heroku master
```

6. **Configuring the Database**: Once deployed, run the database migrations on Heroku:

bash

209

```
heroku run rake db:migrate
```

7. **Configuring Environment Variables**: Set any necessary environment variables using `heroku config:set`. For example, setting a database password:

```
bash
```

```
heroku                                config:set
DATABASE_PASSWORD="mysecretpassword"
```

8. **Opening the Application**: After deployment, you can open your app using:

```
bash
```

```
heroku open
```

This will launch the app in your browser.

9. **Logging**: You can view logs from your Heroku app:

```
bash
```

```
heroku logs --tail
```

210

Deploying on AWS or DigitalOcean: Setting Up Your App on a Cloud Server

While Heroku is a great platform for quick deployments, more control over your infrastructure may require deploying to cloud providers like **Amazon Web Services (AWS)** or **DigitalOcean**. Here's how you can deploy your Rails application on these platforms.

Deploying on AWS (Amazon Web Services)

1. **Set Up an EC2 Instance**: AWS EC2 (Elastic Compute Cloud) provides scalable virtual servers. To deploy Rails to EC2:
   - Log in to the AWS Console and create a new EC2 instance using a **Ubuntu** or **Amazon Linux** AMI (Amazon Machine Image).
   - Choose a **t2.micro** instance type (free tier eligible).
   - Set up security groups to allow HTTP (port 80), HTTPS (port 443), and SSH (port 22).
2. **Set Up the Server**: SSH into the EC2 instance:

bash

```
ssh -i "your-key.pem" ubuntu@ec2-xx-xx-xx-xx.compute-1.amazonaws.com
```

211

Install dependencies on the server:

bash

```
sudo apt-get update
sudo apt-get install git
sudo apt-get install nodejs
sudo apt-get install postgresql
```

3. **Install Ruby, Rails, and Dependencies**: Install **RVM** (Ruby Version Manager), Ruby, and Rails:

bash

```
\curl -sSL https://get.rvm.io | bash -s
stable
rvm install 3.0.0 # install Ruby version
gem install rails
```

4. **Clone Your Application**: Clone your Rails app from GitHub or deploy it via `git`:

bash

```
git clone https://github.com/your-repo/my-
rails-app.git
cd my-rails-app
```

5. **Set Up the Database**: Configure the config/database.yml for PostgreSQL and set up the database:

bash

```
sudo -u postgres createuser --interactive
sudo -u postgres createdb myapp_production
rails db:create
rails db:migrate
```

6. **Set Up Web Server (Nginx and Puma)**: Set up **Nginx** as a reverse proxy and **Puma** as the application server. Install Nginx:

bash

```
sudo apt-get install nginx
```

Configure Nginx to forward requests to your Rails app running with Puma.

7. **Run the Application**: Start the Puma server:

bash

```
bundle exec puma -C config/puma.rb
```

Deploying on DigitalOcean

1. **Set Up a Droplet**: Create a new **Droplet** on DigitalOcean (DigitalOcean's equivalent to a virtual server) using their web interface. You can choose from a variety of Linux distributions, including Ubuntu.

2. **Install Necessary Dependencies**: SSH into your DigitalOcean server and install Ruby, Rails, Node.js, PostgreSQL, and Nginx:

bash

```
sudo apt-get update
sudo apt-get install ruby-full postgresql
nodejs nginx git
```

3. **Set Up the Rails App**: Similar to the AWS setup, clone your Git repository and configure the database. You'll need to ensure that the server is set up with the correct **database credentials** in `config/database.yml`.

4. **Install Web Server**: Install **Nginx** and set it up as a reverse proxy to Puma. Configure Nginx and Puma as described in the AWS section.

5. **Start Your App**: After configuration, start Puma and Nginx to run your application.

Summary

In this chapter, we discussed the steps involved in deploying a Rails application to various environments, including **Heroku**, **AWS**, and **DigitalOcean**. We explored **preparing your app for production** by configuring the production environment, setting up the database, precompiling assets, and configuring security settings. We also walked through **step-by-step guides for deploying to Heroku**, a simple platform for Rails apps, and **AWS/DigitalOcean**, which provide more control and scalability for cloud-based deployments. By following these guides, you can deploy and manage your Rails applications on different cloud platforms, ensuring they are performant, secure, and ready for production.

CHAPTER 20

SECURITY BEST PRACTICES IN RAILS

Common Security Vulnerabilities: CSRF, SQL Injection, XSS

When developing web applications, security is a critical concern. Rails provides many built-in protections to safeguard against common security vulnerabilities. Let's explore some of the most common security risks and how to protect against them.

1. **Cross-Site Request Forgery (CSRF)**: **CSRF** attacks occur when a malicious website causes a user's browser to make unwanted requests to a site where the user is authenticated, potentially performing actions without their consent (such as transferring money, changing settings, etc.).

   How to Prevent CSRF:

   o **CSRF tokens**: Rails automatically includes **CSRF tokens** in every form and verifies that each incoming request includes a valid token.

216

- o In your forms, Rails generates an authenticity token by default:

erb

```
<%= form_for @post do |f| %>
  <%= f.text_field :title %>
  <%= f.submit %>
<% end %>
```

- o This is automatically included in form submissions to ensure that the request is legitimate. If a request is missing or the token is invalid, it will be rejected.
- o **Ensure CSRF protection is enabled**: Rails has CSRF protection enabled by default in ApplicationController:

ruby

```
class ApplicationController <
ActionController::Base
  protect_from_forgery       with:
:exception
end
```

2. **SQL Injection**: **SQL Injection** attacks occur when an attacker can inject malicious SQL code into an

application, potentially gaining access to the database, altering data, or executing arbitrary SQL queries.

How to Prevent SQL Injection:

o **Use ActiveRecord**: Rails' **ActiveRecord** ORM automatically sanitizes inputs, preventing SQL injection. For example:

```ruby
user = User.find_by(email: params[:email])
```

This query automatically escapes `params[:email]` to avoid SQL injection.

o **Avoid raw SQL**: If you must use raw SQL, use parameterized queries to ensure that inputs are safely handled:

```ruby
User.where("email = ?", params[:email])
```

This ensures that `params[:email]` is properly escaped and cannot alter the structure of the SQL query.

3. **Cross-Site Scripting (XSS)**: **XSS** attacks occur when an attacker injects malicious scripts into web pages viewed by other users. This allows attackers to execute JavaScript in a victim's browser, potentially stealing sensitive data or hijacking user sessions.

How to Prevent XSS:

- **Escape Output**: Rails automatically escapes any data that is rendered in views to prevent XSS:

  erb

  ```
  <%= @user.name %> <!-- Automatically
  escapes HTML special characters -->
  ```

- **Use `sanitize` for HTML**: If you allow users to submit HTML content (e.g., in a rich-text editor), use `sanitize` to filter dangerous tags:

  ruby

  ```
  sanitized_content                    =
  sanitize(user_input)
  ```

- **Avoid using `raw` or `html_safe`**: Only use `raw` or `html_safe` when you are absolutely sure that the content is safe and doesn't contain any harmful scripts:

219

```
erb


<%= raw @user.content %> <!-- Use
with caution -->
```

Rails Built-In Security Features: How Rails Helps Protect Your App

Rails comes with many built-in security features to help protect your application from common threats.

1. **Strong Parameters**: Rails uses **strong parameters** to prevent **mass assignment** vulnerabilities, where an attacker could submit data that modifies fields that should be protected (such as an admin role).

   o Strong parameters are automatically enabled when you use `params.require(:model).permit(:fiel d1, :field2)`, which only allows the permitted fields to be passed to the model:

```ruby
def post_params

params.require(:post).permit(:title
, :content)
end
```

2. **Secure Headers**: Rails includes a set of **HTTP headers** to improve the security of your app:

- o **Content Security Policy (CSP)**: Protects against XSS attacks by specifying which sources of content are allowed to be loaded:

```ruby
config.content_security_policy do
|policy|
  policy.default_src :self
  policy.script_src          :self,
'https://trusted.cdn.com'
end
```

- o **HTTP Strict Transport Security (HSTS)**: Forces browsers to only communicate with your app over HTTPS, preventing SSL/TLS stripping attacks:

```ruby
config.ssl_options  =  {  hsts:  {
max_age: 31536000, preload: true } }
```

- o **X-Frame-Options**: Prevents clickjacking attacks by controlling whether your site can be embedded in an iframe:

```ruby
```

```ruby
config.action_dispatch.default_head
ers = {
  'X-Frame-Options' => 'SAMEORIGIN'
}
```

3. **Password Hashing**: Rails uses **bcrypt** by default to securely hash passwords. This prevents attackers from accessing users' plaintext passwords, even if the database is compromised.

   o When creating a new user, use `has_secure_password` to automatically hash the password and authenticate:

   ```ruby
   ```

   ```ruby
   class User < ApplicationRecord
     has_secure_password
   end
   ```

   o To authenticate a user, you can use `authenticate`:

   ```ruby
   ```

   ```ruby
   user       =       User.find_by(email:
   params[:email])
   ```

```
if
user&.authenticate(params[:password
])
  # User is authenticated
else
  # Invalid login
end
```

4. **Session Security**: Rails provides secure cookies and sessions to help protect user data:

   o **Secure Cookies**: Rails uses **signed and encrypted cookies** by default, which prevents tampering and exposure of sensitive information.

   ```ruby
   cookies.signed[:user_id] = @user.id
   ```

   o **Session Expiry**: Rails sessions can be configured to expire after a period of inactivity or a set time, reducing the risk of session hijacking.

Secure Your App: Passwords, Encryption, and Securing User Data

Securing sensitive user data, including passwords and private information, is essential to protect your application from attacks. Here are best practices for securing your app:

1. **Store Passwords Securely**:

   o **Never store plaintext passwords**. Use **bcrypt** (via `has_secure_password`) to hash passwords.

   o Use **PBKDF2** or **Argon2** (available through gems like `argon2` or `bcrypt`) for strong password hashing.

2. **Two-Factor Authentication (2FA)**: Two-factor authentication adds an extra layer of security by requiring users to verify their identity using something they have (such as a phone) in addition to their password.

   Implementing 2FA in Rails involves:

   o Using a gem like **devise-two-factor** or **authy** for easy integration of 2FA features in your Rails app.

3. **Encrypt Sensitive Data**: Rails provides built-in support for encryption with **ActiveRecord Encryption** to securely store sensitive data like credit card numbers or personal information in the database.

   o For example, you can encrypt and decrypt data on the fly:

   ```ruby
   class User < ApplicationRecord
     encrypts :credit_card_number
   ```

```
end
```

- o This encrypts the `credit_card_number` field using a secret key, ensuring sensitive data is protected even in the database.

4. **Use HTTPS (SSL/TLS)**: Always serve your Rails application over **HTTPS** to protect user data in transit. You can enforce HTTPS in production by enabling **HSTS** and redirecting HTTP requests to HTTPS:

```ruby
config.force_ssl = true
```

5. **API Authentication**: When building APIs, it's essential to authenticate requests securely. The most common approach is using **JSON Web Tokens (JWT)** or **OAuth** for token-based authentication:
   - o **JWT Authentication**: This is a popular method for handling stateless authentication in APIs. You can use the `jwt` gem to encode and decode tokens that contain user information.

6. **Secure File Uploads**: If your app allows file uploads (such as images or documents), ensure that files are securely stored and validated:
   - o **Validate File Types**: Ensure that only safe file types (e.g., images, PDFs) are uploaded.

o **Store Files Securely**: Store files outside of the web root, and use cloud services like **Amazon S3** or **Google Cloud Storage** to securely store large files.

Summary

In this chapter, we explored key **security best practices** for Rails applications. We covered common security vulnerabilities such as **CSRF**, **SQL injection**, and **XSS**, and discussed how Rails helps mitigate these risks with features like CSRF protection, SQL-safe queries, and automatic output escaping. We also explored Rails' built-in security features, including password hashing with **bcrypt**, session security, and encryption for sensitive data. Finally, we discussed best practices for securing user data, implementing **two-factor authentication (2FA)**, enforcing **HTTPS**, and securely managing file uploads. By following these best practices, you can protect your Rails application from security vulnerabilities and ensure your users' data is safe.

CHAPTER 21

MANAGING AND SCALING RAILS APPLICATIONS

Performance and Scalability Considerations

As your Rails application grows, it's important to focus on performance and scalability to ensure your app can handle increased traffic and provide a smooth user experience. Performance optimization is about improving the speed and responsiveness of your app, while scalability is about ensuring your app can handle an increasing number of users and requests without degrading performance.

1. **Optimize Database Queries**:
   - o **Use Indexes**: Indexing frequently queried columns can drastically reduce the time it takes to retrieve data from the database. Use the `add_index` migration to create indexes on columns used in search or join queries.
   - o **Avoid N+1 Queries**: Use **eager loading** (`includes`, `joins`) to load associated records in a single query, preventing N+1 query problems. Example:

```ruby
posts                          =
Post.includes(:comments).where(publ
ished: true)
```

- o **Database Query Optimization**: Optimize slow queries by analyzing the query execution plan and considering the use of `select` to limit the fields being returned.
- o **Caching Queries**: Use caching to store frequently accessed data in memory and avoid hitting the database on every request.

2. **Optimize Asset Delivery**:
   - o **Asset Pipeline**: Precompile JavaScript, CSS, and image assets to minimize the number of HTTP requests and reduce load times. Use **gzip** compression for assets in production.
   - o **Content Delivery Networks (CDNs)**: Use a CDN to serve static assets (images, CSS, JS) closer to users, reducing latency and improving load times.

3. **Efficient Background Jobs**: Offload time-consuming tasks to **background jobs** using tools like **Sidekiq** or **Resque**. This allows your app to remain responsive by moving tasks like email sending, file processing, and third-party API calls to background workers.

4. **Minimize Blocking Requests**: Use **non-blocking** I/O, especially for network requests and file uploads. This ensures that your app doesn't hang while waiting for external resources, which can drastically affect performance.

Scaling with Multiple Servers: Load Balancing and Caching

As traffic increases, you may need to distribute the load across multiple servers to handle the demands of users. This can be done through **load balancing**, where incoming requests are distributed across multiple application servers to ensure even traffic distribution. Along with load balancing, caching can be implemented to further optimize your application's performance.

1. **Load Balancing**: Load balancing ensures that no single server becomes a bottleneck by distributing incoming traffic across multiple servers. This is particularly important in production environments where you need to handle large amounts of traffic.

    o **Hardware Load Balancers**: Hardware-based load balancers distribute traffic between application servers at the network level.

    o **Software Load Balancers**: Software solutions like **NGINX**, **HAProxy**, or cloud-based load balancers (e.g., AWS Elastic Load Balancing) can also distribute requests.

- With **NGINX**, you can configure load balancing by defining multiple backend application servers:

```nginx
upstream rails_app {
  server app_server_1;
  server app_server_2;
}

server {
  location / {
    proxy_pass
http://rails_app;
  }
}
```

2. **Horizontal Scaling**: Horizontal scaling involves adding more servers to handle additional traffic. With horizontal scaling, your app can be scaled by simply adding more application instances. This can be done manually or automatically (auto-scaling) in cloud environments like AWS, Azure, or DigitalOcean.

   o **Auto-Scaling**: Cloud platforms like **AWS EC2** or **Heroku** provide auto-scaling, where the

230

number of application servers is automatically adjusted based on traffic demands.

- o **Stateless Servers**: For horizontal scaling to work efficiently, ensure that your application is **stateless**, meaning that each request can be handled independently without relying on the state of the previous requests. Use shared storage (e.g., Amazon S3 for file storage) and databases for storing persistent data.

3. **Caching Strategies for Scaling**: Caching plays a significant role in scaling your application by reducing the number of database queries and improving response times. There are several levels of caching to consider:

- o **Page Caching**: Cache entire pages of the application (especially useful for static content or infrequently changing pages).
- o **Fragment Caching**: Cache parts of the page that are expensive to generate.
- o **Action Caching**: Cache the entire response for a controller action.
- o **Low-Level Caching**: Use **Rails.cache** to cache arbitrary data, such as database query results or expensive computations:

ruby

```
data                        =
Rails.cache.fetch('some_cache_key')
do
  expensive_query_or_computation
end
```

4. Use caching servers like **Memcached** or **Redis** for faster access to cached data.

Database Scaling: Sharding and Replication Strategies

As your app grows and the database becomes a bottleneck, it may be necessary to scale the database. **Sharding** and **replication** are two key strategies for scaling databases effectively.

1. **Database Replication**: **Replication** involves creating copies of your database (replicas) to spread the read traffic. This can significantly increase the read capacity of your application. In replication, one database server (master) is responsible for writing data, while multiple replica servers handle read requests.

   o **Master-Slave Replication**: The **master** database handles all write operations, and the **slave** databases handle read operations. This reduces the load on the master database and ensures that read queries can be distributed.

232

In Rails, you can configure replication in the `config/database.yml` file:

```yaml
yaml

production:
  adapter: postgresql
  database: myapp_production
  username: myapp_user
  password: <%= ENV['DATABASE_PASSWORD'] %>
  host: <%= ENV['DATABASE_HOST'] %>
  pool: 5
  timeout: 5000
  replica:
    host: replica_host
    pool: 5
```

- o **Load Balancing Reads**: By configuring read replicas, you can use **Rails' ActiveRecord** to direct read queries to replicas and write queries to the master database.

2. **Database Sharding**: **Sharding** involves splitting your database into smaller, more manageable pieces called **shards**. Each shard holds a subset of the data. This strategy can improve both read and write performance by distributing the database load across multiple servers.

- o **Vertical Sharding**: Splitting a large database schema into smaller, more manageable chunks (e.g., separate tables for users, orders, and products).
- o **Horizontal Sharding**: Distributing data across multiple databases by partitioning data based on a specific column (e.g., splitting users into different databases by their ID range).

Sharding can be more complex to implement and manage, but it is a powerful strategy for scaling large applications.

3. **Database Partitioning**: Partitioning is similar to sharding but focuses on dividing large tables into smaller, more manageable chunks. For example, a large users table could be partitioned based on the `created_at` column:

- o **Range Partitioning**: Data is partitioned into ranges, such as by year or month.
- o **Hash Partitioning**: Data is distributed based on a hash of a column, such as user ID.

4. **Handling Read/Write Splits**: Rails can handle read/write splitting using **ActiveRecord** and a load balancer for replication, but you'll need to configure it correctly:

```ruby
```

```
ActiveRecord::Base.connected_to(database:
{ writing: :primary, reading: :replica })
```

This ensures that read queries go to the replica database, while write queries go to the primary master database.

Summary

In this chapter, we explored **performance and scalability** considerations for Rails applications. We covered strategies like **load balancing** to distribute traffic across multiple servers and **caching** to improve response times and reduce database load. We also discussed **database scaling** strategies, including **replication** for read-heavy workloads and **sharding** for distributing data across multiple servers. By applying these techniques, you can ensure that your Rails application can scale effectively, handle large amounts of traffic, and provide a fast, reliable experience to users.

CHAPTER 22

WORKING WITH CLOUD SERVICES AND APIS

Integrating with Third-Party Services: Using APIs and Webhooks

One of the most powerful features of modern web applications is the ability to **integrate with third-party services**. Whether you're interacting with payment gateways, social media platforms, email services, or other web applications, **APIs** and **webhooks** are essential for integrating your Rails app with external services.

1. **Using APIs in Rails**: An **API** (Application Programming Interface) allows different systems to communicate with each other. Rails provides several ways to make HTTP requests to third-party APIs, including using the built-in **Net::HTTP** library, **RestClient**, or the more modern **HTTParty** gem.

   Example of using **HTTParty** to interact with an external API:

   o   First, install the gem:

   ```ruby
   ```

```
gem 'httparty'
```

Run `bundle install` to install it.

o   Making a GET request to an API:

```ruby
ruby

class WeatherService
  include HTTParty
  base_uri
"https://api.openweathermap.org/dat
a/2.5"

  def fetch_weather(city)
    self.class.get("/weather",
query:   {   q:   city,   appid:
ENV['OPENWEATHER_API_KEY'] })
  end
end
```

o   You can use the `WeatherService` class to fetch data from the OpenWeather API, providing the city name and your API key as query parameters.

2. **Making POST Requests**: For making POST requests to external APIs (e.g., sending data to a third-party service), you can also use **HTTParty** or **RestClient**:

```ruby
response =
HTTParty.post("https://api.example.com/en
dpoint", body: { key1: "value1", key2:
"value2" }.to_json, headers: { 'Content-
Type' => 'application/json' })
```

- o This sends a POST request to the third-party API with JSON data.

3. **Handling API Responses**: When working with external APIs, you'll typically receive responses in JSON format. Use **Rails' `JSON.parse`** method to convert the response into Ruby objects for easy handling:

```ruby
response =
HTTParty.get("https://api.example.com/end
point")
parsed_response =
JSON.parse(response.body)
```

4. **Using Webhooks**: A **webhook** is a way for an external service to send real-time data to your app via an HTTP POST request. Webhooks are useful for receiving notifications when specific events occur, such as payment completion or new user sign-up.

238

o For example, if you're integrating a payment gateway like **Stripe**, you may set up a webhook to receive events such as payment success:

ruby

```ruby
class         WebhooksController    <
ApplicationController
  skip_before_action
:verify_authenticity_token

  def create
    event                           =
Stripe::Event.construct_from(
      JSON.parse(request.body.read,
symbolize_names: true)
    )

    case event.type
    when 'payment_intent.succeeded'
      # Handle payment success
    when 'payment_intent.failed'
      # Handle payment failure
    end

    render json: { message: 'Event
received' }, status: :ok
  end
end
```

239

- o In this example, the controller listens for incoming POST requests from Stripe and processes the event based on its type.

5. **Securing API Keys**: Always secure your API keys by storing them in **environment variables** or using **Rails credentials** (introduced in Rails 5.2). Avoid hardcoding API keys directly into your codebase.

   - o Example of setting an environment variable:

   ```bash
   export
   OPENWEATHER_API_KEY="your_api_key_h
   ere"
   ```

   - o Accessing the key in your Rails app:

   ```ruby
   ENV['OPENWEATHER_API_KEY']
   ```

   - o Alternatively, use Rails credentials:

   ```bash
   rails credentials:edit
   ```

   - o Accessing in code:

```ruby
ruby
```

```
Rails.application.credentials.openw
eather_api_key
```

Cloud Services: Storing Data in AWS, Google Cloud, etc.

Cloud services are widely used for hosting applications, databases, and storing files. By leveraging services like **Amazon Web Services (AWS)**, **Google Cloud**, or **Microsoft Azure**, you can offload much of the infrastructure management and scale your app with ease.

1. **Using AWS for File Storage (Amazon S3)**: AWS **S3 (Simple Storage Service)** is commonly used for storing large files such as images, videos, and backups. In Rails, you can use the **ActiveStorage** feature to integrate S3 with your app easily.

    o First, add the `aws-sdk-s3` gem to your Gemfile:

    ```ruby
    ruby
    ```

    ```
    gem 'aws-sdk-s3', require: false
    ```

    o Set up **ActiveStorage** to use Amazon S3: In `config/storage.yml`:

    ```
    yaml
    ```

241

```
amazon:
  service: S3
  access_key_id:               <%=
ENV['AWS_ACCESS_KEY_ID'] %>
  secret_access_key:           <%=
ENV['AWS_SECRET_ACCESS_KEY'] %>
  region: 'us-west-2'
  bucket: 'your_bucket_name'
```

o Set ActiveStorage to use S3 in
  `config/environments/production.rb`:

ruby

```
config.active_storage.service   =
:amazon
```

o Now, you can attach files to models using
  ActiveStorage:

ruby

```
class User < ApplicationRecord
  has_one_attached :profile_picture
end
```

In your controller:

ruby

242

```
user.profile_picture.attach(params[
:profile_picture])
```

- o This will automatically upload and retrieve files from Amazon S3.

2. **Using Google Cloud Storage**: Similar to AWS S3, **Google Cloud Storage** can be used for file storage. The google-cloud-storage gem integrates Google Cloud with Rails for storing files.

   - o Add the gem to your Gemfile:

```ruby
gem 'google-cloud-storage'
```

   - o Configure Google Cloud Storage in config/storage.yml:

```yaml
google:
  service: GCS
  project: "your_project_id"
  credentials:
"path/to/your/keyfile.json"
  bucket: "your_bucket_name"
```

   - o Set **ActiveStorage** to use Google Cloud:

243

```
ruby

config.active_storage.service      =
:google
```

o Upload and access files similarly to how you use S3, as demonstrated with **ActiveStorage**.

Building Integrations: Connecting Your Rails App to External APIs

Rails makes it easy to integrate your app with external APIs, whether you're sending data to another service or consuming data from a third-party API. Here's how to build effective integrations.

1. **Sending Data to External APIs**: When sending data to an external API, you can use the **HTTP client** (like **HTTParty**, **RestClient**, or **Faraday**) to make POST requests.

   Example using **HTTParty** to send data:

```
ruby

response                           =
HTTParty.post("https://external-
api.com/endpoint",
```

```
                    body:    {   name:
"John",      email:      "john@example.com"
}.to_json,
                    headers:         {
'Content-Type' => 'application/json' })
```

2. **Consuming Data from External APIs**: When consuming data, you typically send a **GET** request to retrieve data in JSON format. You can parse the response and handle it as needed:

ruby

```
response = HTTParty.get("https://external-api.com/data")
data = JSON.parse(response.body)
```

3. **Handling Errors from External APIs**: When making requests to external APIs, it's essential to handle errors gracefully. For instance, if the API is down or the response is invalid, you should catch the errors and handle them accordingly:

ruby

```
begin
  response                          =
HTTParty.get("https://external-api.com/data")
```

```ruby
raise "Error: #{response.code}" unless
response.success?
  data = JSON.parse(response.body)
rescue StandardError => e
  Rails.logger.error      "API       Error:
#{e.message}"
  # Handle error, e.g., return a default
value or show a user-friendly message
end
```

4. **Webhooks and APIs**: If you need to receive data from an external service in real-time, you can use **webhooks**. For example, if an external service sends a webhook notification when an event occurs, Rails can listen for and process those events by implementing a controller that handles incoming POST requests.

Example of a controller handling a webhook:

```ruby
ruby

class          WebhooksController          <
ApplicationController
  skip_before_action
:verify_authenticity_token

  def create
    data = JSON.parse(request.body.read)
    # Process the data
```

```
    end
  end
```

Summary

In this chapter, we covered how to **integrate with third-party services** using **APIs and webhooks**, how to **store data in cloud services** like **AWS** and **Google Cloud**, and how to **build integrations** by connecting your Rails app to external services. By using APIs and webhooks, you can enhance your Rails application's functionality by leveraging powerful external services. Whether you're integrating payment gateways, sending data to external systems, or storing large amounts of data in the cloud, Rails makes it easy to connect and scale your app using these technologies.

CHAPTER 23

VERSION CONTROL AND COLLABORATION WITH GIT

Why Version Control is Essential

Version control is a critical aspect of modern software development. It enables developers to track and manage changes to their codebase, making it easier to collaborate, maintain code integrity, and manage releases. Without version control, keeping track of changes, managing different versions of the code, and resolving conflicts among team members becomes cumbersome and error-prone.

1. **Key Benefits of Version Control**:
   - o **Tracking Changes**: Version control systems (VCS) like **Git** allow you to track all changes made to the codebase, including who made the change, when it was made, and why. This helps to maintain a history of changes and allows for easy rollback to previous versions if necessary.
   - o **Collaboration**: Multiple developers can work on the same project simultaneously without

interfering with each other's work. Git handles merges and conflict resolution.

- o **Backup and Recovery**: Since code is stored in a version control system, you always have a backup of the entire history of your project. If something goes wrong, you can roll back to a previous stable version.

- o **Branching and Experimentation**: Git allows you to create branches to experiment with new features or bug fixes without affecting the main codebase. This makes it easy to try out new ideas and test changes in isolation.

2. **Git as the Standard VCS**: Git has become the de facto standard for version control in the software development world due to its speed, flexibility, and widespread adoption. Unlike centralized version control systems (like SVN), Git is **distributed**, meaning every developer has a full of the repository on their machine. This allows for offline work and faster operations.

Using Git with Rails: Best Practices

When using Git with a Rails application, adhering to best practices helps ensure smooth collaboration, maintainability, and a clean, organized repository.

249

1. **Set Up Your Git Repository**: To initialize a Git repository in your Rails project:

bash

```
git init
```

Then, create a `.gitignore` file to specify which files and directories Git should ignore. For Rails, this file typically includes:

bash

```
/log/*
/tmp/*
/db/*.sqlite3
/public/assets/*
/.byebug_history
/node_modules/*
/vendor/bundle/*
```

The `.gitignore` file helps to keep unnecessary or sensitive files (e.g., database files, logs, or temporary files) out of the repository.

2. **Commit Frequently and with Meaningful Messages**: Commit often with meaningful commit messages to make it easy to track changes:

```
bash
```

```
git add .
git commit -m "Add user authentication system"
```

A good commit message should describe the "what" and the "why" of the change. Avoid vague messages like "Fixed bug" or "Updated code."

3. **Branching for Features and Bug Fixes**: Always use **branches** for new features, bug fixes, or experiments. This keeps the `main` branch (or `master` branch) stable and clean.

   o To create and switch to a new branch:

   ```
   bash
   ```

   ```
   git checkout -b feature/login-system
   ```

   o After completing work on the branch, merge it into the `main` branch:

   ```
   bash
   ```

   ```
   git checkout main
   git merge feature/login-system
   ```

4. **Avoid Large, Monolithic Commits**: Each commit should represent a logical unit of work. Avoid committing unrelated changes together. If you're working on multiple tasks, break them into separate commits to make it easier to track changes and resolve issues.

5. **Use `git rebase` to Keep a Clean History**: When working in teams, you may need to rebase your branch onto the latest version of the `main` branch to avoid unnecessary merge commits:

bash

```
git fetch origin
git rebase origin/main
```

This re-applies your commits on top of the current `main` branch, keeping the history linear and clean. However, be cautious when rebasing shared branches, as it rewrites commit history.

6. **Check the Status and Diff Regularly**: Use `git status` to check the status of your working directory and `git diff` to view changes you've made before committing:

bash

```
git status
git diff
```

252

Collaborating with Teams Using GitHub: Code Reviews, Pull Requests, and Branching Strategies

GitHub is one of the most popular platforms for hosting Git repositories. It provides tools to manage collaboration, including code reviews, pull requests, and branching strategies.

1. **Forking and Cloning Repositories**:
   o When working with open-source projects or external repositories, you can **fork** a repository to create a personal of the project.
   o Clone the forked repository to your local machine:

   bash

   ```
   git clone https://github.com/your-
   username/project-name.git
   ```

2. **Using Pull Requests (PRs)**: A **pull request** (PR) is a way to submit changes to a repository. PRs allow other team members to review your code before merging it into the main branch.
   o After pushing your branch to GitHub, you can create a PR from the GitHub interface. A good PR should include:
     ▪ A clear description of what changes are being made and why.

- Any relevant information such as how to test the changes or known limitations.
  - **Code Review Process**: Team members review the PR, suggest changes, and approve or request further changes before it is merged. The reviewer checks for things like coding standards, test coverage, and logic errors.

3. **Branching Strategies**: A solid **branching strategy** helps maintain a clean, organized project and ensures smooth collaboration. Common strategies include:
   - **Feature Branches**: Each new feature is developed in its own branch. This keeps features isolated and prevents developers from stepping on each other's toes.
     - Example: `feature/user-authentication`
   - **Bug Fix Branches**: Bug fixes should be handled in their own branches to avoid mixing them with feature development.
     - Example: `bugfix/fix-login-issue`
   - **Git Flow**: This strategy is based on multiple long-running branches:
     - `main`: The stable, production-ready branch.

- develop: The integration branch where features are merged before being released to production.
- feature/*: Branches for new features.
- release/*: Branches for preparing releases.
- hotfix/*: Branches for critical production fixes.

4. **Rebasing vs. Merging in PRs**:
   o **Merging** creates a merge commit and is ideal for larger features or when you want to keep a record of when and how features were integrated.
   o **Rebasing** re-applies your commits on top of the latest main branch and can keep the commit history clean, but it should be used cautiously with shared branches.

When collaborating on PRs, it's best practice to use **rebase** to keep the commit history linear and clean:

bash

```
git pull --rebase origin main
```

5. **Handling Merge Conflicts**: Merge conflicts happen when two branches make changes to the same line of code. Git will prompt you to resolve these conflicts

255

manually. After resolving conflicts, mark the file as resolved:

```bash
```

```bash
git add <conflicted-file>
git commit
```

Summary

In this chapter, we covered the essentials of **version control** using **Git**, emphasizing its importance in modern software development. We explored best practices for using Git with Rails, including how to structure your repository, commit frequently, and manage branches for new features or bug fixes. Additionally, we discussed how to **collaborate with teams using GitHub**, focusing on **code reviews**, **pull requests**, and **branching strategies**. By following these best practices, you can ensure smooth collaboration, maintain code quality, and effectively manage your Rails application's development lifecycle.

CHAPTER 24

ADVANCED TOPICS AND FUTURE OF RAILS

Upcoming Features in Rails: What's New in Rails 7 and Beyond

The Ruby on Rails community is constantly evolving, and with each new release, Rails introduces new features and improvements that enhance development speed, performance, and maintainability. Rails 7, released in December 2021, introduced several exciting updates that make Rails more modern, efficient, and flexible.

1. **Hotwire (HTML Over The Wire)**: Rails 7 introduced **Hotwire**, a framework for building modern, interactive applications without using heavy JavaScript frameworks like React or Vue. Hotwire consists of two parts:
   - **Turbo**: Turbo enables you to make parts of your application dynamic by sending only the necessary HTML over the wire. This improves performance by reducing the need for full-page reloads.
   - **Stimulus**: Stimulus complements Turbo by providing a minimal, reactive JavaScript

framework that enhances interactivity without the complexity of larger libraries.

Hotwire allows you to build real-time, dynamic features like live updates and user interactions using only server-side code and minimal JavaScript.

Example of using Turbo:

```erb
<%= link_to 'Show Post', post_path(post),
data: { turbo_frame: 'post' } %>
```

This will replace only the content of the `post` frame without reloading the entire page.

2. **Asynchronous Querying with async**: Rails 7 introduced built-in support for **asynchronous queries** in ActiveRecord. With the `async` keyword, you can perform long-running queries without blocking the main thread. This can significantly improve performance for applications that require fetching large amounts of data.

Example:

```ruby
posts = Post.async.where(published: true)
```

258

3. **Defaulting to Webpacker for JavaScript**: Rails 7 has made **Webpacker** the default for managing JavaScript assets. Webpacker allows Rails developers to manage JavaScript dependencies, and it integrates seamlessly with modern JavaScript tools, frameworks, and ES6 modules.

4. **Improved Active Storage**: Rails 7 comes with improvements to **ActiveStorage**, making it easier to handle file attachments. New features like **direct uploads** and better integration with cloud storage services such as Amazon S3, Google Cloud Storage, and Microsoft Azure make managing file storage simpler and more efficient.

5. **Better Multithreading**: Rails 7 has improved multithreading support to help Rails applications scale more efficiently. By leveraging Ruby's native threading model, Rails apps can handle more requests concurrently, which is especially beneficial in resource-intensive applications.

6. **Enhanced Security Features**: Rails 7 introduces better security features, such as defaulting to **HSTS** (HTTP Strict Transport Security), enabling **secure cookies**, and enforcing **content security policies**. These improvements help to mitigate common web security vulnerabilities, such as Cross-Site Scripting (XSS) and Cross-Site Request Forgery (CSRF).

7. **Support for HTTP/2 and HTTP/3**: Rails 7 supports **HTTP/2** and **HTTP/3**, which provide better performance for modern web applications. These protocols enable faster loading by allowing multiplexing, server push, and header compression.

8. **JIT (Just-In-Time) Compilation for Ruby**: Rails 7 benefits from **Ruby's JIT compiler**, which improves the performance of Rails applications by compiling Ruby code into machine code during runtime. This results in faster execution of Ruby code, making Rails apps more responsive.

Advanced Topics: Service Objects, POROs, and Advanced Patterns

As you gain more experience with Rails, you'll encounter patterns and techniques that allow you to build scalable, maintainable applications. Here are some advanced topics that can significantly improve your Rails codebase.

1. **Service Objects**: **Service objects** are plain Ruby classes that encapsulate business logic that doesn't belong in models, controllers, or views. By using service objects, you can keep your codebase clean, organized, and easy to test.

Service objects are useful for tasks like:

- o Processing complex business logic.

- o Interacting with external APIs.

- o Orchestrating workflows across different models or services.

Example:

```ruby

class CreateUser
  def initialize(user_params)
    @user_params = user_params
  end

  def call
    ActiveRecord::Base.transaction do
      user = User.create!(@user_params)
      # Send welcome email
      # Perform other tasks
      user
    end
  rescue ActiveRecord::RecordInvalid => e
    # Handle error
  end
end
```

To use the service object:

```ruby
```

```
service = CreateUser.new(user_params)
service.call
```

2. **POROs (Plain Old Ruby Objects)**: **POROs** are simple Ruby objects that are not tied to any specific Rails component (e.g., ActiveRecord, ActionController). They allow you to encapsulate logic without coupling it to the Rails framework.

POROs are useful for tasks like:

- Representing domain models that do not require persistence.
- Encapsulating complex logic outside of models and controllers.

Example of a PORO:

```ruby
ruby

class Money
  attr_reader :amount

  def initialize(amount)
    @amount = amount
  end

  def add(other_money)
```

```ruby
      Money.new(amount + other_money.amount)
    end
end
```

In this example, the `Money` class encapsulates money-related logic without depending on Rails.

3. **Query Objects**: **Query objects** are used to encapsulate complex queries in a separate object, keeping controllers and models clean. They help in building reusable, readable, and testable database queries.

   Example:

   ruby

```ruby
class FindPostsByCategory
  def initialize(category)
    @category = category
  end

  def call
    Post.where(category:
@category).order(created_at: :desc)
  end
end
```

   You can then use the query object like this:

   ruby

```
posts                                    =
FindPostsByCategory.new('Tech').call
```

4. **Form Objects**: **Form objects** are used to handle form submissions that involve multiple models. Instead of putting logic for multiple models in a single controller or form view, you can use a form object to encapsulate the logic.

Example:

```ruby
class SignUpForm
  include ActiveModel::Model
  attr_accessor :user_name, :email, :password, :password_confirmation

  validates :user_name, :email, presence: true
  validates :password, confirmation: true

  def save
    return false unless valid?

    user = User.create!(user_name: user_name, email: email, password: password)
```

```
        user
    end
end
```

Contributing to the Rails Community: How to Get Involved in Rails Development

Contributing to the **Rails community** is a great way to learn more, share your knowledge, and help improve the framework. Here are ways to get involved in Rails development:

1. **Contributing to the Rails Codebase**:
    o **Fork and Clone the Repository**: Start by forking the official Rails GitHub repository, cloning it to your local machine, and setting up your development environment.
    o **Fix Bugs or Add Features**: Browse the Rails GitHub issues to find bugs or feature requests that you can work on. Start with simple issues or documentation improvements if you're new to contributing.
    o **Submit Pull Requests (PRs)**: After making your changes, submit a pull request for review. Be sure to write clear commit messages, follow the Rails coding style, and provide tests for your changes.

Rails follows a strict code review process. Your PR will be reviewed by core maintainers, and they may ask for changes or improvements.

2. **Testing and Reporting Bugs**:
   - o Rails is always evolving, and testing the framework on your own applications can help identify bugs. If you find an issue, report it to the Rails GitHub repository with as much detail as possible.
   - o Join the community discussions to talk about potential improvements, bugs, or new features.

3. **Participating in Rails Events**:
   - o Attend **RailsConf** and **RubyConf**: These conferences provide opportunities to learn, network, and contribute to the Rails ecosystem.
   - o Join Rails-related communities on **Slack**, **Discord**, or **Reddit** to engage with other developers and participate in discussions or events.

4. **Rails Plugins and Gems**:
   - o Build and maintain **Rails plugins** or **gems**. Contributing useful gems to the community is a great way to improve the ecosystem and showcase your skills. You can publish gems to **RubyGems.org** and integrate them into your projects or other Rails applications.

266

5. **Writing Articles or Tutorials**:

   o Writing blog posts, tutorials, or creating video content can help new Rails developers and showcase your expertise. Contributing educational resources is another way to give back to the community.

6. **Participating in Discussions and Feature Proposals**:

   o Rails has an official mailing list and discussion forum where new features and ideas are discussed. Join the conversation and participate in proposals for new Rails features. If you have an idea for an improvement, you can start a discussion on **GitHub Discussions**.

Summary

In this chapter, we explored the **future of Rails**, focusing on the exciting new features in **Rails 7** and beyond, including Hotwire, Turbo, and asynchronous querying. We also discussed **advanced topics** in Rails development, such as service objects, POROs, and other design patterns that help keep your code clean and maintainable. Finally, we covered how to **contribute to the Rails community**, whether through contributing code, reporting bugs, attending events, or writing tutorials. By staying involved, you can deepen your Rails expertise, share your knowledge, and help improve the framework for developers worldwide.

www.ingramcontent.com/pod-product-compliance
Lightning Source LLC
LaVergne TN
LVHW022338060326
832902LV00022B/4111